# Acclaim for *Seventy '...*

**Dick Staub,** Host, *The Dick Staub Show,* WYLL/Chicago
A fine book on a subject that virtually everyone of us wrestles with. These honest and touching stories – many of them based on personal experiences of the author and his parents – model forgiveness in a profound way…and provide lessons to pass on to the next generation.

**Philip Yancey,** author, *The Jesus I Never Knew*
What a treasure trove of stories Arnold has given us! As a concept, forgiveness challenges our primal instincts of justice and fairness. Jesus' commands to forgive seem idealistic and impractical – until one reads these stories and realizes the supernatural power of forgiveness, a power available to every one of us.

**Madeleine L'Engle,** author, *A Wrinkle in Time*
Beautiful…Arnold illumines his theology with many examples, including instances where the wound is deep and it is not easy to forgive. He understands that true forgiveness is an act of God's grace, which we must be willing to receive, rather than a mere act of the will.
We recognize ourselves in the poignant stories, and our recognition helps us to forgive. This is a book the whole world needs.

**Myron Augsburger,** author, *The Peacemaker*
Biblical, relevant, and psychologically insightful. A remarkable book on the freedom and healing that comes from forgiveness.

**Benedict J. Groeschel,** C.F.R., Archdiocese of New York
With his customary blend of Gospel faith and personal sharing, Arnold invites us to explore and resolve the hurts and bitterness that we all experience in life. This is spiritual reading at its best.

**Fidel Castro**
An important work on a theme of significance for all humankind.

**David Bercot,** author, *The Pilgrim Road*
Outstanding, interesting throughout, and readable…

**Lewis Smedes,** author, *The Art of Forgiving*
> Arnold has written a book so simple, so transparent, so caring, and so lovely that all who read it will delight in it...they will also be led tenderly into the healing grace that all who have been wronged by another so much need.

**Mohammed T. Mehdi,** National Council on Islamic Affairs
> *Seventy Times Seven* reflects the spirit of the forgiving Creator, which should be the direction of all people on earth.

**Michael Henderson,** author, *The Forgiveness Factor*
> These stories are an inspiration and a challenge. Taken seriously, the message of *Seventy Times Seven* will help us prepare for the next millennium.

**Molly Kelly,** National lecturer on teen issues
> A moving testimony to the power of forgiveness that may change lives...Forgiveness is the key to healing, and this book gives people the key.

**Judson M. Procyk,** Metropolitan Archbishop of Pittsburgh
> Refreshing, dramatic, and heartwarming examples of the power of forgiveness...Arnold beautifully develops and reinforces the understanding that when a person forgives from the heart, true reconciliation and healing follow.

**Arun Gandhi,** M.K. Gandhi Institute
> In our haste to condemn we have lost the art of forgiving. *Seventy Times Seven* takes us to the depths of spirituality and show us how divine it is to forgive.

**John Michael Talbot,** musician, writer
> A most compelling and challenging book for Christians and non-Christians alike...based on solid Biblical traditions and the author's own experience. The testimonies contained in the book show that Arnold's ideals are not mere theory, but can be lived – and have been.

**Paul Brand, M.D.,** author, *Pain: The Gift Nobody Wants*
> This is the book I would choose to give to friends who are justifiably angry at someone who has harmed them...It is a powerful statement on the centrality of forgiveness in the Christian faith and its importance generally in human psychology.

**Everett L. Worthington,** Virginia Commonwealth University

In moving and thought-provoking stories, Arnold demonstrates a central truth of Christianity: that evil *can* be overcome by good... This is not a theology text. It is life.

**George W. Kosicki,** C.S.B., Divine Mercy International

Beautifully illustrates the truth of the Sermon on the Mount and the Lord's Prayer: that in marriage and in community, the condition for receiving God's gift of mercy is being merciful and forgiving one another.

# SEVENTYTIMESSEVEN

# SEVENTY
# TIMES
# SEVEN

## The Power of Forgiveness

**Johann Christoph Arnold**

Foreword by J. I. Packer

**The Plough Publishing House**

©1997 by The Plough Publishing House
of The Bruderhof Foundation

Farmington PA 15437 USA
Robertsbridge, E. Sussex, TN32 5DR  UK

Cover photograph: © Pete Turner / Image Bank 1997

The photograph on page 73 is reprinted by permission
of Newsday, Inc. © 1997 Newsday, Inc.

Library of Congress Cataloging-in-Publication Data

Arnold, Johann Christoph, 1940 –
    Seventy times seven : the power of forgiveness / Johann Christoph
Arnold.
        p.   cm.
    Includes bibliographical references.
    ISBN 0-87486-092-X (pbk.)
    1. Forgiveness--Religious aspects--Christianity.   2. Bruderhof Com-
munities--Discipline   I. Title.
    BV4647.F55A76   1997
    234'.5--dc21                                          97-30774
                                                             CIP

Printed in the USA

To MY WIFE, Verena,
without whose loving support
none of my books could have been written.

# Acknowledgments

IT WOULD TAKE more than a page to list everyone who helped bring this book into print – there are dozens who worked on it, from those who typed the first draft to those who did the final layout and designed the cover. I thank each one, especially Reuben Zimmerman, my editor, but also Emmy Maria Blough, Hanna Rimes, Ellen Keiderling, Hela Ehrlich, Chris Zimmerman, Emmy Barth, Dan Hallock, Emily Alexander, and Clare Stober.

Many people gave me valuable advice as I worked on the manuscript. I would especially like to thank three: Sr. Ann Laforest, whose thoughtful critiques have now helped shape all four of my books; her sister Frances Kieffer; and Fr. Benedict Groeschel, whose enthusiasm and friendship have encouraged me to keep writing.

Most of all I would like to acknowledge those who allowed me to use their stories: Anne Coleman, Marietta Jaeger, Bill Chadwick, Steven McDonald, Chris Carrier, Elias Chacour, Bishara Awad, Naim Ateek, Marie Wilson, Joel Dorkam, John Plummer, and Michael Ross – not to mention many fellow members of my community, the Bruderhof. Your willingness to share has given this book a compelling personal dimension, and I am grateful to each of you.

Several of the names in this book were changed to protect contributors' identities. Where a first name appears without a surname, it is a pseudonym; all other names are real.

# Contents

# Foreword

*Peter came to Jesus and asked, "Lord, how many times shall I forgive my brother when he sins against me? Up to seven times?" Jesus answered, "I tell you, not seven times, but seventy times seven."* Mt. 18:21–22

Readiness to forgive, Jesus taught his disciples, is the acid test of our moral and spiritual stature, and indeed of whether we are real Christians or not. As personal experience constantly shows, nothing withers the soul more than an unforgiving spirit – the poisonous product of pain and pride that craves revenge under the guise of justice. Forgiveness is as important, searching, and demanding a theme as any a Christian can write about.

The author of this book is a pastor in a community movement that has a heritage of nonviolent witness, an international membership, and a prophetic purpose of challenging many assumptions about life that the secular and Christians worlds too often take for granted.

There is much discernment, much authority, and much food for thought in what Arnold has written, and in the personal stories that he includes. This is a book to be read, reread, and pondered deeply.

J. I. Packer
*Regent College, Vancouver*

IF YOU LOVE only those who love you, what reward can you expect? Surely the tax gatherers do as much as that. And if you greet only your brothers, what is extraordinary about that? Even the heathen do as much. There must be no limit to your goodness, just as your heavenly Father's goodness knows no bounds.

*Jesus of Nazareth*

# CHAPTER ONE

ONE MORNING in September 1995, as I sat drinking coffee and reading the local paper, I was horrified to see headlines reporting the abduction, in broad daylight, of a local seven-year-old girl. Over the next few days, I followed the story closely.

Within a week the girl was found in a wooded area only several hundred yards from the county jail, raped, sodomized, and beaten to death. Even worse, the man who admitted to the crime turned out to be an acquaintance of the child – and one she trusted.

The public's reaction was predictable: this man deserved to die. Under the state's new capital punishment statute, he was a prime candidate. Although the district attorney had promised a maximum of twenty years in exchange for the body, he went back on his word only days later, saying that he would have made a pact with the devil to find the child, and that he hoped to become the first DA in recent New York history to send a murderer to the death chamber. Residents interviewed in the local paper even suggested that he be released on the street so they could "take care of him."

While this rage was understandable, I wondered how it could possibly bring solace to the victim's grieving family. As a minister, I felt fairly certain what my response should be: I sent representatives from my congregation to the funeral, and flowers to the child's parents. I tried, unsuccessfully, to visit the family. But my heart still felt heavy. Somehow, I knew I had to visit the murderer – at this point still a faceless monster – to confront him personally with the horror of his deed, and to urge him to repent.

I knew people would look askance at such a visit, if not misunderstand it entirely, but I was convinced it was my duty. So it was that a few months later I found myself sitting alone in the county jail, face to face with the uncuffed killer. The hours I spent in that cell shook me deeply and left many unresolved questions – questions, in fact, that eventually led me to write this book. Why should I or anyone forgive this man? What would it change? Didn't he first have to show remorse? And even if he did, would I have the right to forgive him, since he hadn't hurt me?

Less than three months after my visit, the murderer finally faced his victim's family. The county courthouse was packed, and entering it, one could feel a wave of hostility. The sentence – life imprisonment without parole – was followed by a statement from the judge: "I hope that the hell you now face in prison is only a foretaste of the hell you will face in eternity."

The defendant was then allowed a few words. In a loud, wavering voice, he told the girl's parents that he was "truly sorry" for the pain he had caused – and that he prayed daily for forgiveness. As a ripple of angry whispers spread through the audience, I asked myself the hardest question of all: can such a man ever be forgiven, anyway?

THE MAN who opts for revenge should dig two graves.

*Chinese proverb*

THOUGH JUSTICE be thy plea, consider this:
That in the course of justice none of us
Should see salvation. We do pray for mercy,
And that same prayer doth teach us all to render
The deeds of mercy.

*William Shakespeare*

# CHAPTER TWO

FORGIVENESS IS THE WAY to peace and happiness. It is also a mystery, and unless we seek it, it will remain hidden from us. This book is not intended as a theology of forgiveness – it is impossible to tell someone how to forgive – but I do hope it can help to illustrate why forgiveness is needed. Forgiveness *is* possible. In the following stories I will try to lead you to its door. Once there, only you can open it.

What does forgiveness really mean? C.S. Lewis says it is not just human fairness; it is excusing those things that can't readily be excused at all.[1] In a way, it is even more than that. When we excuse someone, we brush his mistake aside and do not punish him for it. When we forgive, we not only pardon a failing or sin, but we embrace the sinner and seek to rehabilitate and restore him. Our forgiveness may not always be accepted, yet once we have reached out our hand, we cleanse ourselves of resentment. We may remain deeply wounded, but we will not use our hurt to inflict further pain on others.

When we re-visit a negative memory in the sense of chalking up another person's wrongs to us, it becomes a grudge. It doesn't matter if the cause of the grudge is real or imagined: once there, it will slowly eat away at us until it spills out and corrodes everything around us.

We all know bitter people. They have an amazing memory for the tiniest detail, and they wallow in self-pity and resentment. They catalog every offense against them and are always ready to show others how much they have been hurt. On the outside they may appear to be calm and composed, but inside they are bursting with pent-up hatred.

These people defend their indignation constantly: they feel that they have been hurt too deeply and too often, and that somehow this exempts them from the need to forgive. But it is just these people who need to forgive most of all. Their hearts are sometimes so full of rancor that they no longer have the capacity to love.

Almost twenty years ago, my father and I counseled such a woman. Her husband lay dying, yet she was as hard and unfeeling as a rock. In the eyes of the world, she had lived a blameless life: she was neat and meticulous, hard-working, honest, capable, and dependable – yet she could not love. After months of struggle, the cause of her coldness became clear: she was unable to forgive. She couldn't point to a single large hurt, but she was bowed down by the collective weight of a thousand small grudges.

Bitterness is more than just a negative outlook on life. It is a sin. To willfully hold on to grudges against another person has a disastrous effect on the soul. It opens the door to evil and leaves us vulnerable to thoughts of murder. In addition, it renders our prayers powerless; this is why Christ commands us to settle our differences with others before we "offer our gifts at the altar." We can pray all day, but if we harbor grudges, the door to God will remain closed.

Bitterness destroys our souls, and it can destroy our bodies as well. We know that stress can cause an ulcer or a migraine, but we fail to see the relationship between bitterness and insomnia. Medical researchers have even shown a connection between unresolved anger and heart attacks; it seems that people who bottle up their resentment are far more susceptible than those who are able to defuse it by venting their emotions.

NOT LONG AGO I was asked to help a young woman who had been sexually abused by her uncle. Although she was without question the innocent victim of a horribly depraved man, her misery seemed at least in part self-perpetuated. She would not and could not muster enough inner strength to forgive.

Silenced for years by fear of exposure and by her alcoholism, which her tormentor supported with daily gifts of vodka, this poor woman cried out to me in despair. She had been offered intensive psychiatric counseling, and she lacked nothing in material comforts. She had a good job and an extensive network of supportive friends, and every effort in the world had been made to get her back on her feet. In spite of this, her emotions swung widely, from excited laughter to inconsolable weeping. She binged on food one day and fasted and purged the next. And she drank – bottle after bottle.

This needy soul was perhaps one of the most difficult people I have ever tried to help. I was extremely hesitant to burden her with even one ounce of guilt, yet it seemed clear to me that only she could initiate the healing process. But all our counseling seemed to be in vain. Angry and confused, she drove herself deeper and deeper into despair, and finally, after attempting to strangle herself, she had to be hospitalized.

The wounds left by sexual abuse take years to heal; often, they leave permanent scars. Yet they need not result in life-long torment or in suicide. For every case like the one I have just described, I know of others where victims have found freedom and new life by forgiving. This does not mean forgetting or condoning – certainly it does not depend on a face-to-face meeting with a former abuser, which may be inadvisable. But it does mean making a conscious decision to stop hating, because hating can never help. Like cancer, it can spread through a person till it completely destroys him.

Daniel            Anne            Frances

Anne COLEMAN, a mother from Delaware whom I met at a conference several months ago, told me what happened to her son Daniel, who could not forgive:

> When my daughter Frances was murdered in 1985, I was devastated. I received a phone call from my niece in Los Angeles, and she said, "Frances is dead; she's been shot."
>
> I can't remember screaming, but I did. I made plans to go out to California immediately, and on the plane I really thought I could kill someone: if I'd had a weapon and the murderer, I probably would have done just that.
>
> By the time I got off the plane I was getting concerned about how I was going to greet my son Daniel, who was flying in from Hawaii. Daniel was an army sergeant, and he had been trained to kill...
>
> When we got to the police station the next morning, the only thing they told us was that my daughter was dead, and that everything else was none of our business. Sadly, this remained the case throughout the days we

stayed in Los Angeles. The violent crimes coordinator told me that if they hadn't arrested someone in four days, I shouldn't expect an arrest: "We just have too many homicides in this precinct – we spend only four days on homicides."

This enraged my son Daniel. When he found out that the police department was really not interested in finding his sister's killer, he wanted to go buy an Uzi and mow people down...

They hadn't really prepared us for what we would see when we picked up her car from the pound. Frances had bled to death in her car. The bullets had passed through her aorta, her heart, both lungs. She had choked on her own blood. She died early on a Sunday morning, and we picked up the car late Tuesday afternoon. It stank. That smell never left Daniel's mind, and he wanted vengeance in the worst way. He really wanted someone to do something – some kind of justice for his sister.

Over the next two-and-a-half years I saw Daniel go downhill, and then I stood alongside his sister's grave to watch him being lowered into the ground. He had finally taken revenge – on himself. And I saw what hatred does: it takes the ultimate toll on one's mind and body.

LOOKING DOWN into my father's
dead face
for the last time
my mother said without
tears, without smiles
but with *civility,*
"Good night, Willie Lee, I'll see you
in the morning."
And it was then I knew the healing
of all our wounds
is forgiveness
that permits a promise
of our return
at the end.

*Alice Walker*

# CHAPTER THREE

MANY OF US will never be faced with forgiving a murderer. But all of us are faced daily with the need to forgive husband or wife, children, colleagues – perhaps dozens of times in a single day. And this task is no less important.

In his poem "A Poison Tree," William Blake shows us how the smallest resentment can blossom and bear deadly fruit:

> I was angry with my friend:
> I told my wrath, my wrath did end.
> I was angry with my foe:
> I told it not, my wrath did grow.
>
> And I water'd it in fears,
> Night and morning with my tears;

And I sunned it with smiles,
And with soft deceitful wiles.

And it grew both day and night,
Till it bore an apple bright;
And my foe beheld it shine,
And he knew that it was mine,

And into my garden stole
When the night had veil'd the pole:
In the morning glad I see
My foe outstretched beneath the tree.

The petty grudges of everyday life are the seeds to Blake's tree. If they fall into fertile hearts, they will grow, and if they are tended and nurtured they will take on a life of their own. They may be small, seemingly insignificant, even hardly noticeable at first, but they must nonetheless be overcome. Blake shows us in the first two lines how easily this can be done: we must face our anger immediately and root it out before it grows.

I had to learn not to hold on to grudges early in my life. My childhood was a happy one for the most part, but I had my share of unpleasant experiences. I was a sickly child. Soon after I was born the doctors told my mother that I had hydrocephalus or "water on the brain," and that I would never walk. Even though this did not prove to be true – I did walk at two-and-a-half – the nickname "waterhead" stuck. This hurt my parents the most, but it affected me as well.

I was also lonely. There were seven children in our family, but I was the only boy. In addition, my father was gone for three of the first five years of my life. So I longed for friends.

When I was six, I had to have a large tumor removed from my leg. This was the first of many such operations over the next three decades. The surgery lasted two hours, and the threat of infection – this was before the days of antibiotics, and we were living in the backwoods of Paraguay – hung over me for days. After my leg was stitched shut, I walked home from the hospital. No one offered me crutches, let alone a wagon. I can still see my father's shocked face as I limped into our house, though he didn't say a thing.

That was typical of my parents. We never heard them speak ill of others, and they did not allow us to, either.

Christoph Arnold with his parents, 1957

Like any other parents, they struggled with their feelings when they felt one of us children had been mistreated by a teacher or other adults. But they insisted that the only way to overcome the little indignities of life was to forgive.

When I was fourteen, we moved to the United States. The change from a village in the South American wilderness to a public high school in New York was enormous. The English language was certainly a barrier for me, but I was also shy because I felt I was awkward and clumsy. Every child wants to be recognized by his peers – no one wants to be left behind – and I was no different. I desperately wanted to be accepted, and I went out of my way to please my new classmates. At first I was spurned, especially by a boy who had the reputation of being a bully, but then I began to fight back. My friends were all émigrés like myself, and we mocked him mercilessly, speaking German among ourselves, which he didn't understand. Our animosity led to more than a few bloody noses.

In high school I went out for cross-country running. I gave it my best and never missed practice, but I just wasn't good enough. Still, the coach realized how hard I was trying, and his friendship did wonders for my self-esteem. He encouraged me to try out for track, which I did. In the end, though I was never a star athlete, I made the team.

In my twenties I dealt with feelings of rejection when I sought the friendship of a young woman. Our relationship deepened and we became engaged, but then one day suddenly she turned her back on me. (I was sure it was because I was such an awkward misfit.) A few years later I became interested in another woman, though this time I held back cautiously. For a second time my hopes were dashed: after several months she, too, broke off our relationship. My world crashed around me and I tried to make

**Christoph and Verena Arnold, May 1966**

sense of what had happened. What had I done wrong?

It took me a long time to get over my hurt and rebuild my confidence. But my father assured me that in God's time I would find the right person, and this proved to be true when some years later I found my wife, Verena.

It is less difficult to forgive a stranger than a person we know and trust. This is why it is so hard to overcome betrayal by close friends or colleagues. They know our deepest thoughts, our frailties, our quirks – and when they turn on us, we are left reeling.

Pete, a friend from Virginia, recently shared one such experience with me:

> Before moving to another state and leaving my business, I had to settle affairs with my partner of ten years. This was complicated by the fact that he and his wife were very close to me; we had been in the same small Christian fellowship for the past fifteen years.
>
> No one would advise me about how best to make an equitable settlement of our business assets. I wanted to be not only fair, but generous. I wanted nothing hang-

ing on my conscience. And so I came up with a division that would give me half of the earnings to the date I left, and leave them with the other half, the jobs in progress, and the equity and good will of the business with which to continue. But they saw the whole thing otherwise and stopped talking to me the day I gave notice. Unfortunately, I had given two-months' notice, so the transition was long, silent, and lonely, punctuated only by angry words.

At the time I left we still had not signed an agreement. Lawyers had been brought in by both of us, but they only clouded the waters. I had wanted an outside source who could tell them to accept my fair offer. But they fired the lawyer and sought counsel from an accountant we had worked with for seven years. I'm not sure just what happened, but he quickly lost his objectivity and began to work against me.

It took a lot of writing and counter-offering to finally come to an agreement. They insisted that even though I was to be paid off by December, they would not be able to mail the check until December 31. Only later did I learn that this delay made me liable for one-half of our earnings for the entire year – even though I had only received my share of the earnings through June. I ended up paying $50,000 in taxes. I was so angry I could not sleep for days. I felt totally betrayed by this "Christian" brother and his "Christian" accountant, whom I felt had conspired to crush me.

I really had to reach deep to forgive that one. But somehow the grace was given and then I realized that I needed to write and ask their forgiveness, too. I felt such a release as I licked the envelope and put the letter in the mail. No matter what their answer, I needed to be free of my anger.

About a month later, a friend of mine who had counseled me to forgive called to ask if I had been able to do so. I told her that I had, and she answered, "I thought so; I've noticed a real freeing in him, too."

UNFORTUNATELY, BETRAYAL by friends or colleagues is common in many so-called Christian circles. As a pastor at the Bruderhof, my father was known and respected for his ability to comfort and counsel. Wherever he went, people lined up to speak to him. Many had confessions to make; others needed pastoral advice or just a listening ear. For whatever reason, he was envied for this and hated as much as he was praised.

Papa had suffered from kidney problems around the time I was born, and as I grew up these problems became worse. Life in Paraguay was harsh; disease was rampant, and the fight to survive was made harder by tensions in our group. The burden of Papa's pastoral responsibilities weighed on him as never before. At one point, after several weeks of steady physical decline, his doctors told him he had only forty hours left to live. Fearing the worst, he summoned the entire membership of the church to his bedside, where he exhorted them to prayer and steadfastness in this wilderness so far from home. He also passed on his leadership and pastoral duties to three other members, one of them his brother-in-law.

**Heinrich and Annemarie Arnold, 1958**

Papa miraculously recovered, but to his surprise the community's leaders told him that his days as a minister were over: the doctor had declared him too weak to continue such demanding work. The main reason, they said, was the "emotional instability" he had displayed at the height of his illness, when he had had bizarre dreams and hallucinations. Papa gave in and began to work in our small missionary school and hospital.

Though my parents did not realize it at the time, this turn of events was no accident. It had been calculated (and the doctor's words twisted) in an attempt to bar him from his life's calling. In actual fact, the doctor had suggested only a few weeks of additional rest. It was only thirty years later that another doctor discovered and explained to him the real reason for his hallucinations – the expected side-effect of his primitive bromide medications. Never once, however, did we children feel bitterness on his part.

It wasn't long, though, before new problems surfaced in our church. My parents, concerned about a spreading wave of legalism, and feeling that Christ and his love was being replaced by human rules and regulations, joined a handful of other members in trying to raise an opposing voice, but they were misunderstood. Accused of "leading a faction," several of them were sent away, including Papa, who was left once again without a job. Although a skilled gardener (he had studied horticulture in Zurich) he was unable to find work of any kind: he was suspect to Paraguay's German settlers, who tended to be sympathetic to the Nazis, and British and American expatriates feared him simply because he was German. Finally, he found employment as a farm manager in a leper colony.

In the early 1940s no cure existed for leprosy, and such work was extremely dangerous. He was warned of contagion, and was told by more than one doctor of the danger that he might never see his wife or children again. The anguish he suffered is hard to describe.

I will never forget my excitement the day Papa returned from the leper colony. Straddling his shoulders as he strode toward the house, I called out, "Papa is home!" to every passerby. But for the most part, we were met with icy stares.

It was years before I found out the real reason for Papa's expulsion: he had felt that the leaders of our church were too autocratic, repressive, and cold-hearted, and when he had pleaded with them for more compassion and understanding, they had accused him of "emotionalism."

Papa did not become bitter, however. More than once he said that Christ's suffering is of no use unless we are willing to suffer with him. He also pointed out how much better it is to trust others and risk betrayal than to live in fear and mistrust.

I was already in my twenties when I first heard these stories from my father's older friends. I was horrified. How would I react if I were pushed aside by fellow ministers without explanation?

In 1980 I found out. My church suddenly asked me to step down from my work as assistant elder to my father, a task I had been appointed to almost ten years earlier. To this day I am not completely sure why it happened. Certainly there was an element of the same divisive jealousy that had hurt my parents forty years earlier, but this time it was my friends, colleagues, and siblings who for the most part turned against me. All of a sudden, the very same people who had always praised and encouraged me began to find fault with everything I had ever done.

Confused and angry, I was tempted to fight back. My father was then senior elder of four large congregations, and he needed me more than ever; only weeks before, my mother had died of cancer. I desperately wanted to set my record straight and reestablish my "rightful" place.

Papa, however, refused to support me in fighting back. Instead he pointed me to the Sermon on the Mount, where Jesus speaks of forgiving others for their trespasses so that we, too, may be forgiven. He reminded me that in the

end we won't have to answer for what others do to us –
only for what we do to them.

Suddenly I realized I wasn't as good as I had thought I
was. I began to see that deep down I held grudges against
certain members of my community, and that instead of
trying to justify myself, I needed to get down on my knees
and ask God to forgive me. Then I would find strength to
forgive. As soon as I did this, my struggle took on a wholly
new meaning. I felt as if a dam had burst open somewhere
deep down inside my heart. Before, I had felt the pain of
hurt pride; now I could ask myself: What does it matter in
God's eyes?

With a new determination to set things straight and to
take the blame for whatever tensions existed, I went with
my wife to people we felt we had hurt in the past and
asked them to forgive us. As we went from one to another,
we felt God at work, and our hearts became lighter.

That year was a very painful one for me and my wife,
but it was also an important one. It prepared us for the
responsibilities we carry now by giving us a greater sense
of compassion for others. And it taught us some lessons we
will never forget. First, it does not matter if people misunderstand you or accuse you unjustly; ultimately, what mat-
ters is that your heart is right before God. Second, though
the decision to forgive must always come from within, we
cannot change in our own strength. The power of forgiveness comes not from us, but from God. He can work in us
only when we turn to him in prayer, trust, and humble
recognition of our weaknesses.

J IM AND CAROLYN WEEKS, members of our community since the mid-1970s, went through hard times the same year. They, too, found that forgiveness is the only way to reconciliation. Carolyn writes:

Jim and Carolyn Weeks with their daughter Veronica, 1983

In 1980 we had already been living at the Bruderhof for five years. We were convinced God had called us, and we badly wanted to become full members. But it was a time of chaos and uncertainty, and when we couldn't understand things, we easily became upset by them, and ended up backing ourselves into a corner.

Finally we decided to ask for a retreat, a few weeks' leave from the community so that we could work things out on our own and find peace with our brothers and sisters. Unfortunately, our request was misunderstood, and we ended up leaving the community as if for good. I will never forget driving away. Some of our friends came out to say good-bye, but all I could feel inside was a great emptiness.

How could this have happened? Only weeks before we had been certain we would soon be permanent members of the Bruderhof, and now all our dreams were shattered. We had sacrificed everything to join this way of life. As a young married couple we had come with some of our wedding gifts still wrapped. We had given the community our car and everything else we owned.

The Bruderhof took good care of us materially, providing us with a truckload of furniture and even a driver to carry us to our new home in Baltimore, yet we still struggled with feelings of abandonment and rejection. We felt as though we were miserable failures. We tried to block out all our memories – there had been happy times – and threw ourselves into our new life.

It took us eight years to recover financially, with plenty of help from family and friends. By this time we had come to accept our lot. Both of us had secure jobs, the kids were enrolled in good schools with plenty of friends, and we were only a few years away from paying off our mortgage. But inside we were empty and lonely, and we knew something was missing. Initially, we had talked about trying to return to the Bruderhof, but after a few years we gave up on this hope completely. And although we didn't know it, we built up a great wall of bitterness in our hearts.

Then one morning about ten years after we had left, the phone rang just as our kids were getting on the school bus. It was a couple from the Bruderhof who were in town and wanted to see us. At first we were apprehensive, but then the inevitable happened: we invited them for dinner. We were friendly but hesitant to get involved. Even though we hadn't sorted out all of our feelings, we knew we had been deeply hurt. So the couple left, and we didn't see anyone from the Bruderhof again until several months later, when we visited "just for one weekend."

We ended up coming back for a second weekend, and we were invited to a special members' meeting to explain our position and to set the record straight, so

that at the very least we could once again be friends.
The meeting started out fine, but by the end of it we
realized to our great shock that the minister whom we
had trusted the most had in fact understood us the least.
That hurt. After that meeting, we were still willing to be
friends with the community, but no more than that.

Imagine our surprise, then, when the next morning
this minister and his wife drove two hours to see us, to
ask us for our forgiveness. When we heard that they had
come, we didn't want to see them at first; we were too
afraid of what we might say. Then we reluctantly agreed
to talk to them. To our amazement, they met us with
open arms and eyes filled with tears. They said they
were sorry and held out their hands as a greeting of
peace. What a moment! After all they had done to us,
after ten years of nightmares, after all we had been
through, how could we ever start again? Here they were,
ten years older, but otherwise unchanged – and they
weren't holding back.

We wanted to hold back, but we couldn't. Our hands
went out to theirs, and we forgave them…Within
months we were back at the Bruderhof.

Once Jim and Carolyn returned home, it wasn't long before they began to see that they, too, were not without
guilt. They write, "We had to see that there were two sides
to the story – that we had been obstinate and opinionated,
and that our pride was an obstacle to reconciliation."

Very few disputes are one-sided. In our pride, however,
we see only the sins of others and are blind to our own
faults. Unless we are able to humble ourselves, we cannot

forgive or be forgiven. This humbling is painful, but it is an inevitable and inescapable part of life. Forgiveness allows us to move beyond this pain, even as we acknowledge it, to the joy that comes from love. M. Scott Peck writes:

> There is no way that we can live a rich life unless we are willing to suffer repeatedly, experiencing depression and despair, fear and anxiety, grief and sadness, anger and the agony of forgiving, confusion and doubt, criticism and rejection. A life lacking these emotional upheavals will not only be useless to ourselves; it will be useless to others. We cannot heal without being willing to be hurt.[2]

True community, whether with our spouse and family, our spiritual brothers and sisters, or with our colleagues or friends, demands that we bare our souls to each other. C. S. Lewis goes so far as to say that "to love at all is to be vulnerable. The only place outside Heaven where you can be perfectly safe from all the dangers and perturbations of love is Hell."[3]

Jim and Carolyn's story shows plainly, however, that forgiveness can bring people back together. Hard times, if overcome, can lead to greater love. They can strengthen rather than weaken the bond of unity.

WE HAVE ALREADY SEEN where the cultivation of small grudges leads. Almost always, this cultivation takes the form of gossip. We complain to others about our hurts in order to gain sympathy, and in doing so we add fuel to the fire and spread our resentments further.

If we look at society today – at our homes and schools, hospitals and churches, offices and factories – it is not hard to see the devastating effects of gossip: lost work time and decreased productivity, stress and burnout, and even suicide. How can this evil be overcome?

Difficult as it may be, the only way to rid ourselves of anger and release pent-up feelings in an honest and straightforward manner is direct speaking.

Eberhard Arnold, my grandfather and co-founder of the Bruderhof, felt so strongly about the importance of this that he formulated it as a "rule of love" which he encouraged each member to hang at his place of work. Over the decades we have held to this rule, which is derived from words of Jesus in Matthew 18, and recognized its importance again and again:

There is no law but love. Love is joy in others. What, then, is anger with them? Words of love convey the joy we have in the presence of our brothers and sisters. It is out of the question to speak about another person in a spirit of irritation or vexation. There must never be talk, either in open remarks or by insinuation, against a brother or a sister or against their individual characteristics – and under no circumstances behind their back. Gossiping in one's family is no exception.

Without this rule of silence there can be no loyalty and thus no community. Direct address is the only way possible; it is the spontaneous brotherly or sisterly service we owe anyone whose weaknesses cause a negative reaction in us. An open word spoken directly to another person deepens friendship and is not resented. Only when two people do not come to agreement quickly in a direct manner is it necessary to draw in a third person whom both of them trust. In this way they can be led to a solution that unites them on the highest and deepest levels.[4]

Nineteenth-century theologian and pastor J. Christoph Blumhardt suggests that sometimes it may be best to forgo direct confrontation and simply forgive. This is especially vital when our resentment has no proven cause – if, for example, it is based on a second-hand remark. Otherwise we may remain sullen and mistrustful forever, waiting for an apology that can never be made.

All of us have wronged (or have been wronged by) others at some point in our lives. Yet to dwell on human failings is to deny the power of love and forgiveness. The Spirit can move in our lives if we only open our hearts to it. Love is greater than hatred; faith is greater than doubt; and hope is greater than despair.

Five hundred years ago Thomas à Kempis advised fellow monks that "our peace in this life should depend on humble forbearance rather than on the absence of adversity."[5] This forbearance, which is willingness to forgive, is the secret, the oil or balm of a truly happy life. Without forgiveness we will never find real community with God, nor lasting relationships with each other. With it, our lives will be more richly blessed than we can ever imagine.

THERE IS A HARD LAW…that when a deep injury is done to us, we never recover until we forgive.

*Alan Paton*

PEOPLE ASK ME what advice I have for a married couple struggling in their relationship. I always answer: pray and forgive. And to young people from violent homes, I say: pray and forgive. And again, even to the single mother with no family support: pray and forgive.

*Mother Teresa*

# CHAPTER FOUR

OVER MANY YEARS of counseling, I have seen again and again that unless husband and wife forgive each other daily, marriage can become a living hell. I have also seen that the thorniest problems can often be resolved with three simple words: *I am sorry.*

To ask one's spouse for forgiveness can be difficult. It requires humility and the acknowledgment of weaknesses and failures. And yet just this is what makes a marriage healthy: both partners live in mutual humility, fully aware of their inner dependence on each other. Dietrich Bonhoeffer writes that we must "live together in the forgiveness of sins," because without forgiveness no human fellowship – and least of all a marriage – can survive: "Don't insist on your rights, don't blame each other, don't judge or condemn each other, don't find fault with each other, but accept each other as you are, and forgive each other every day from the bottom of your hearts."[6]

In thirty-one years of marriage Verena and I have had no lack of opportunities to test our willingness to forgive. Only a week after our wedding we had our first crisis. My sister, an artist, had made us a beautiful set of dishes. We had invited my parents and sisters over to dinner in our new apartment, and Verena had spent all afternoon cooking. I set the table with my sister's crockery. My family arrived and we sat down to eat. Suddenly both ends of the table collapsed – I had not snapped the hinged extensions properly into place. Food and broken pottery covered the floor, and my wife fled the room in tears. It was hours before we could laugh about this disaster, though it has now become a family legend.

By the time we had eight children there were plenty of reasons for disagreement. Every evening, Verena would bathe the children, dress them in clean pajamas, and they would wait for me on the couch with their favorite books. When I came home from work, however, they wanted to play, and sometimes we ended up romping in the yard. Verena still remembers the hours she spent removing grass stains and mud – and not without a little grumbling!

Most of our children suffered from asthma, and when they were small they woke us almost nightly with their coughing and wheezing. This, too, brought discord between us, especially when she reminded me that I could get out of bed and attend to them just as well as she.

We had plenty of arguments over my work as well. As a salesman for our publishing house I spent countless days on the road, and because my territory covered western

**Christoph and Verena Arnold and their children, 1978**

New York – Buffalo, Rochester, and Syracuse – I was often a good six or eight hours' drive away from home. My traveling only increased with time. As my father's assistant, I traveled to Europe several times a year, and later as Elder I made frequent trips to Canada, Europe, and even Africa. Almost always, I ended up defending such trips as "vitally important," even though this assertion did little to soothe my wife, who packed my suitcases, adjusted herself to a hectic schedule, and often stayed behind with the children.

Then there was the *New York Times*. After a hard day on the road, I couldn't see the harm in stretching out with the paper for a few minutes while the children played happily around me, and I voiced this opinion rather vehemently. Only later did I come to see my selfishness.

I often think about how our marriage might have turned out if we hadn't learned to forgive each other on a daily basis right from the start. So many couples sleep in the same bed and share the same house but remain miles apart inwardly because they have built up a wall of resentment between themselves. The bricks in this wall may be very small – a forgotten anniversary, a misunderstanding, a business meeting that took precedence over a long-awaited family outing. Wives bristle when their husbands drop laundry onto the floor instead of into the hamper, and husbands can't take it when their wives remind them that they, too, have been working all day.

Many marriages could be saved by the simple realization that people are imperfect. Too often, couples assume that a "good" marriage will be free of arguments and disagreements. Unable to live up to this unrealistic expectation, they become quickly disillusioned; before long, they separate on grounds of incompatibility.

Human imperfection means that we will make mistakes and hurt each other, unknowingly and even knowingly. And in my life, the only fail-safe solution I have found is to forgive, if necessary seventy times seven in one day, and to pray. Without praying together on a daily basis, the myriad tensions that are part of every marriage may simmer needlessly. An active prayer life, on the other hand, can keep a couple focused on God and thus protect their unity. C. S. Lewis writes:

> To forgive the incessant provocations of daily life – to keep on forgiving the bossy mother-in-law, the bullying

husband, the nagging wife, the selfish daughter, the deceitful son – how can we do it? Only, I think, by remembering where we stand, by meaning our words when we say in our prayers each night, "Forgive our trespasses as we forgive those who trespass against us." We are offered forgiveness on no other terms. To refuse it is to refuse God's mercy for ourselves. There is no hint of exceptions and God means what He says. [7]

THE POWER OF PRAYER is wonderfully illustrated by the story of my wife's parents, Hans and Margrit Meier. Hans was a strong-willed man, and his stubbornness caused more than one period of separation in their marriage. An ardent anti-militarist, he was imprisoned only months after their wedding in 1929 because he refused to join the Swiss army.

Shortly after his release, the couple was separated again. Margrit, who had just discovered the Bruderhof and was visiting there, wanted to join the community; Hans, a religious socialist with very different ideas about communal life, did not. Margrit had recently given birth to their first child, and she begged him to join them, but Hans could not be easily swayed. It was several months before she convinced him to come.

Thirty years and eleven children later, Hans and Margrit separated again. By this time they were living in South America; it was 1961, and a time of great internal confusion and upheaval at the Bruderhof.[8] Unable to see his own

**Hans and Margrit Meier on their 50th wedding anniversary, May 11, 1979**

failures – or to forgive those of others – Hans became estranged both from his wife and from the community. In the aftermath, Margrit and the children emigrated to the United States. Hans dug in his heels and settled in Buenos Aires, where he remained for the next eleven years.

There were no signs of outward rancor, but there were no signs of healing either. Slowly, a wall of bitterness rose up and threatened to keep them apart forever. When I married Hans and Margrit's daughter Verena in 1966, Hans did not even attend the wedding, and our children began to grow up without a grandfather on their mother's side.

In 1972 I traveled to Buenos Aires with Verena's brother, Andreas, in an attempt to reconcile with their father. But Hans wasn't interested – at least not at first. He only wanted to recount his side of the story and let us know once again how many times he had been hurt. On the last day of our trip, though, something changed. He announced that he would visit us in the United States. He insisted that he would come for just two weeks, and emphasized the fact that he had a return ticket. But it was an opening.

When the visit finally materialized, we were disappointed. Hans simply could not forgive. We made every effort to clear up the difficulties of the past and acknowledged our guilt in the events leading up to his long estrangement, but we weren't getting anywhere. Intellectually, Hans knew that the only thing standing between us was his inability to forgive. Yet he could not humble himself enough to do this.

Then came the turning point. In the middle of a members' meeting, my uncle Hans-Hermann, who was dying of lung cancer, summoned all his strength, walked up to Hans, and tapped him on the chest saying, "Hans, the change must happen here!" These words cost a tremendous effort: Hans-Hermann was receiving supplemental oxygen through nasal tubes and was barely able to speak. Hans was completely disarmed. His coldness melted away, and he decided then and there to return. After traveling back to Argentina to wind up his affairs, he moved back to join Margrit and the community and soon proved to be the same dedicated, energetic member he had been decades before.

In all his years away, Hans never touched another woman. During that same long decade, Margrit prayed daily for her husband's return. All the same, both had been hurt, and it took time for them to rebuild their trust in one another. As their son-in-law, I can testify that they did: they lived in love and joy with each other and their children, grandchildren, and great-grandchildren until Margrit's death sixteen years later.

EVEN IF WE FORGIVE someone who has truly hurt us, isn't it only human to remain indignant at what they have done? This is a difficult question, but perhaps it has more to do with our difficulty in upholding a human sense of justice than with forgiving. As Hans and Margrit discovered, forgiveness is more than justice. It is a gift. And to those who cannot accept it, it may seem irrational or stupid.

The story of my parents-in-law shows that even long separations can be healed. But can a marriage damaged by adultery or abuse ever be fully repaired? Jesus says it was because of hard-heartedness that Moses allowed divorce, but that among his disciples this can no longer be a valid excuse. Christ's love reconciles and forgives, whereas those who divorce and then remarry close the door to future chances of reconciliation. Even if circumstances dictate a temporary separation, faithful love is the only way to healing and reunion.

The enormous breach of trust caused by infidelity can take years to heal. At first it may be necessary for the partners to live separately, so that each can receive counseling under the guidance of someone they both trust. Then they must be willing to work toward rebuilding their trust so that the marriage can be restored.

When I began writing this book I had just begun counseling a couple whose marriage was destroyed by adultery. Ed and Carol were married nine years ago. Already before he was married, Ed was a problem drinker, and from the start his alcoholism brought great tensions to the marriage. Although they remained together in the same house, inwardly they drifted further and further apart. Some years into their marriage, Ed began a secret affair with a neighbor. During this time, Carol found herself becoming more and more depressed, though she never knew why.

Ed and Carol first came to the Bruderhof in the mid-1990s, and within days Ed told his wife about his affair. In spite of the fact that we knew nothing about it, he felt his sin was somehow being confronted, and his guilty conscience gave him no peace. Carol was dumbfounded. She had sensed for a long time that something was wrong, but she had never imagined such deception. Justifiably angry, she told Ed that their marriage was over, and that she could never forgive him.

It wasn't hard to sympathize with her emotions, but I knew from the start that the only way to healing would be just that: to forgive. I tried to help her see that to accept defeat would only drive them further apart and deny God the possibility of ever bringing them together again.

At the same time, though, I advised an immediate separation with counseling for both partners. Such a separation is biblical: according to the gospel, for a couple to live together while one partner lives in adultery only perpetuates the same sin (1 Cor. 6:15–16). In addition, it would help both Ed and Carol come to terms with their emotions on their own. There could be no "quick fix," and the process would be long and painful. A new relationship had to be built from the bottom up.

Ed and Carol were separated for several months, but during this period both of them made remarkable progress in their relationship. At first they communicated by phone calls only. Later their conversations grew longer and more relaxed, and they began to visit each other as well. Ed stopped drinking, and slowly the joy and freedom that follow repentance began to replace the agony of months of soul-searching. Carol struggled with plenty of hard moments, but she was eager to start over. Soon she felt a new love for Ed, and began to pray for him daily with their children, who had stayed with her when Ed moved out of the house. Most important, she was willing to fully forgive him. Once she recognized that she herself bore a certain guilt for their estrangement, she was able to humble herself and meet Ed on his level.

Now, ten months later, Ed and Carol are together again. In a special service held to celebrate their new start, they publicly forgave each other and re-founded their marriage. Then, faces beaming, they exchanged new rings.

Ed and Carol are not the first couple I have counseled through the heartache of adultery, and they may not be the last. Yet I am confident that other couples, too, will find strength to weather even this storm, as long as both partners are willing to seek renewal on the basis of mutual forgiveness and love.

IT MAY BE INFINITELY WORSE to refuse to forgive than to murder, because the latter may be an impulse of a moment of heat, whereas the former is a cold and deliberate choice of the heart.

*George Macdonald*

WHEN YOU LOVE PEOPLE, you see all the good in them, all the Christ in them. God sees his Son in us. And so we should see Christ in others, and nothing else, and love them. There can never be enough of it. There can never be enough thinking about it. St. John of the Cross said that where there was no love, put love, and you would draw love out.

*Dorothy Day*

# CHAPTER FIVE

NOT ALL STORIES have tidy endings. What about the murderer who is never apprehended or the marriage partner who runs away, never to be seen again? We may not always be able to confront the person we need to forgive, and even if we do, he or she may not be repentant.

Jennifer, a longtime acquaintance, lost her fiancé when he left her ten days before their wedding date, and she never saw him again. They had been engaged for more than a year, and although the relationship had occasionally faltered, she was sure that this time everything was going to work out. She was deeply in love, and very excited. She had finally graduated from nursing school, and her wedding dress was nearly finished. Then everything fell apart:

> My fiancé revealed that he had been dishonest with me – there were things in his past that were still an obstacle to our marriage. To make things worse, he wanted

to run away from it all rather than confront his past. I was shattered. I wept for days and was heartbroken for years. I blamed myself for his dishonesty, and I became bitter.

Thirty years later, Jennifer is still single, but she is no longer bitter. Even though she cannot tell him, she has forgiven her fiancé, and although she sometimes still aches for the marriage that never was, she has found fulfillment in serving others – the old and the sick, expectant mothers, and disabled children. Few of her friends know about her past. Happy and energetic, she is too busy to entertain self-pity:

Because I am single, I can do things a busy wife and mother could never do. I can give of myself whenever and wherever I am needed. And I have cared for and loved more children than I ever could have otherwise.

Is Jennifer a saint? Or can others like her find forgiveness, and through it, peace of heart? At first glance, one might be tempted to conclude that it is next to impossible to give up marriage involuntarily. But does happiness in life really depend on having a spouse and children? To be sure, a family can bring one unfathomable joy, but there is much in married life that can cause grief as well. I have often seen greater dedication in single people than in men and women who are tied down to their families.

Perhaps Jennifer's story can give hope to others who have been abandoned by someone they loved. Certainly it should comfort those who search for a life of commitment and dedication, that is, a life lived in single-minded service to Christ.

JULIE, a woman who joined the Bruderhof in the mid 1980s, left our community with her husband and children after she confronted him for molesting their daughter. The couple hoped that away from the community they could refocus their relationship and gather as a family unit, but unfortunately things didn't work out that way.

> I was foundering on the verge of desperation. My husband had become a stranger to me, and I could no longer live with him in what had become a hell. We had spent a whole year away from the community, hoping to save our marriage and our family, but now it was no use. Everything was lost.
>
> I left him and returned to the Bruderhof, angry, hurt, hateful, rejected, despairing, outraged, humiliated – even this long string of adjectives cannot express what I felt. A battle raged in my heart. I wanted to forgive, but I also wanted to lash out in revenge, and every time I thought of his new wife (he had divorced me and re-married), it rekindled my emotions. It has not been an easy battle, and it continues still, as I witness the effect on our five children.
>
> Wanting to forgive – this was my battle: to genuinely want to forgive him. I knew this should be my response. I could not read the Bible or pray without being confronted by this imperative. But how could I forgive him

when he was so unrepentant, and what was the practical expression of my forgiveness?

I didn't want to gloss over what he had done in any way, but I decided that the most loving thing I could do was to accept the divorce, to pray for him – though I also let him know that I could not allow my children to stay with him any longer.

I have since discovered that forgiving him was not a one-time thing. I must affirm my forgiveness again and again. Sometimes I doubt that I have ever forgiven him at all, and then I have to battle through that, too.

In the end, it is God's faithfulness that I cling to, because I know that ultimately, the wrongs my husband has done to me cannot separate me from God. I need only worry about the wrongs I have done to others.

Julie's story illustrates a vital point: even if her former husband never repents, she must forgive. If she did not, she would remain bound to him by her bitterness, and he would continue to influence her thoughts and emotions. She would remain wounded by what was done to her and her children for the rest of her life. Yet by letting go of her anger and hatred, by realizing that bitterness is wasted energy, she has found new strength to love her children and move on.

WHEN MARIETTA Jaeger's seven-year-old daughter was kidnapped from their tent during a camping trip in Montana, her initial reaction was one of rage:

I was seething with hate, ravaged with a desire for revenge. "Even if Susie were brought back alive and well this minute, I could kill that man for what he has done to my family," I said to my husband, and I meant it with every fiber of my being.

Justifiable as her reaction was, Marietta says she soon realized that no amount of anger could bring her daughter back. Not that she was ready to forgive her daughter's kidnapper: she told herself that to do that would be to betray her daughter. She "wrestled" with God. Yet finally she surrendered: deep down inside, she sensed that forgiving him was the only way she would ever be able to cope with her loss.

As she prayed for the kidnapper over the weeks and months that followed, her prayers became easier and more earnest. She simply had to find the person who had taken away her beloved child. And she even felt an uncanny desire to talk with him face to face.

Then one night, a year to the minute after her daughter had been abducted, Marietta received a phone call. It was the kidnapper. Marietta was afraid – the voice was smug and taunting – but she was also surprised at her strange but genuine feeling of compassion for the man at the other end of the line. And she noticed that, as she calmed down, he did too. They talked for over an hour.

Luckily Marietta was able to record their conversation. Even so it was months before the FBI finally tracked him down and arrested him, and it was only then that she knew her daughter would never come home. The investigators had found the backbone of a small child among the kidnapper's belongings.

State law offered the death penalty, but Marietta was not out for revenge. She writes: "By then, I had finally come to learn that God's idea of justice is not punishment, but restoration…Jesus did not come to hurt or punish, but to rehabilitate and reconcile." Later she requested that her child's killer be given an alternative sentence of life imprisonment with psychiatric counseling. The tormented young man soon committed suicide, but she never regretted her decision to offer him help. Her efforts at

Marietta and Susie Jaeger, the day before Susie was kidnapped

peacemaking did not end there. Today, she is part of a group that works for reconciliation between murderers and the families of victims.

I HAVE ALREADY WRITTEN of Anne Coleman's son Danny and his tragic death. This second loss changed Anne's life. Today she counsels men on Delaware's death row. Anne's work began when she first met Barbara Lewis, a woman whose son was on death row. After visiting Barbara's son together, they began to visit other inmates as well:

So I met Billy. He'd had no visitors, and he was very lonely. And I cry when I think of how he was hanged; how they made him stand on the gallows in that howling wind for at least fifteen minutes while they waited for the witnesses to arrive...After his execution I thought I couldn't go on. But it was prayer that carried me through.

Then I got to know a little boy called Marcus. His father is also on death row. He has no mother and has lost both of his sisters, and he has nightmares because now he's going to lose his father, too.

I know that hating someone is not going to bring my daughter back. And at this point, I don't know if I'll ever find the person who killed her, anyway. But one has to find healing somehow, and I've found it by helping the Barbaras and Marcuses of this world. Helping them has given me more healing than I ever imagined.

IT IS FREEING to become aware that we do not have to be victims of our past and can learn new ways of responding. But there is a step beyond this recognition…It is the step of forgiveness. Forgiveness is love practiced among people who love poorly. It sets us free without wanting anything in return.

*Henri J. M. Nouwen*

# CHAPTER SIX

MANY PEOPLE TODAY struggle to find healing from a broken past. Countless lives have been deeply wounded by childhood abuse – psychological, physical, and, worst of all, sexual. Television shows and magazines deal with these themes on a daily basis. On one program after another survivors pour out their painful stories to a jaded and uncaring public. Yet it seems that no amount of soul-baring brings them the healing they seek. How can they find it?

Ronald grew up on an Appalachian farmstead in western Pennsylvania. Forty or so family members shared the same house, trying to eke a living from the land. His childhood was brutal: he tells of cousins who tried to hang one another and a grandmother who fired at disobedient children with a shotgun full of rock salt.

Ronald's father was an intelligent man though, and eventually he left the farm with his children and moved to Long Island, where he found work. His finances improved, but his relationships did not. His wife left him, and he routinely beat his children, sometimes severely. Ronald lived in constant fear of the violence that awaited him each day when he returned home from school.

Then his father was badly injured in an automobile accident. His neck was broken, and he was paralyzed from the neck down. Once the tyrant of the household, he was now a paraplegic, utterly dependent on others to care for his daily needs.

As a young adult, Ronald had every reason to abandon his father. Why should he stay and care for the man who had ruined his life? Yet he has never left his father's side. Although medical and disability benefits provide some nursing help, he takes on most of his father's care himself. For years he has faithfully seen to his father's daily needs – washing, dressing, and exercising the lifeless limbs that once beat him mercilessly, sometimes to the point of unconsciousness. Often he takes him outdoors in his wheelchair, and they talk about the emotional battles they have both fought and are still fighting.

Demons of the past still haunt Ronald on occasion, but he says he has finally found a measure of the peace he so sorely missed in his childhood. More than anything else, his loving service attests to the forgiveness and healing both he and his father now feel.

**Karl Keiderling, early 1920s**

KARL, a member of our communities who died in 1993, also suffered a harsh childhood. The only son of a German working-class family, his early years were clouded by the First World War and the economic devastation that followed it. His mother died when he was four and his stepmother when he was fourteen. After her death, his father put an ad in the paper that intentionally excluded Karl: "Widower with three daughters looking for a housekeeper; possibility of future marriage."

Several women applied, and in the end one decided to stay. It was only afterwards that she found out about the existence of a boy in the house, and she never quite forgave her new husband for withholding this from her. Karl's food was always poorer than the rest of the family's, and she complained about him constantly.

Karl's father, for his part, was silent in the face of his new wife's stern, unfeeling manner and did nothing to defend his son. In fact, he joined her in mistreating the boy and often beat him with a leather strap mounted with brass rings. When Karl tried to protect himself, his father would only grow more furious and hit him over the head and in the face.

As soon as he could, Karl left home. Attracted by the youth movement sweeping the country in those postwar years, he joined ranks with atheists and anarchists and others who believed that they must change the world, and set out to make sure that society would never be the same again. He wandered through Germany until he came across the Bruderhof, where he responded immediately to the love he felt and decided to stay. He threw himself vigorously into life at the community, but his childhood experiences didn't leave him. Again and again his resentment toward his parents hung like a heavy weight on his heart. Finally, he went to my grandfather and poured out his anger and hatred.

The response was startling: he suggested that Karl write to his parents and ask their forgiveness, to set right the times when he had consciously hurt their feelings or caused them grief. He told Karl to look only at his own guilt, not at theirs. At first Karl was taken aback, but he did as he was advised. His father acknowledged his letter, and although he never apologized for any of the wrongs he had done, Karl's burden was lifted. For the first time in his life he was able to find peace, and he never complained about his childhood again.

MARY, A FRIEND of our family's, overcame painful memories of abuse in a similar way:

My mother died at the age of forty-two, leaving behind

my father and eight children, ages one through nineteen. This loss was devastating for our family, and my father broke down emotionally just when we needed him most. He tried to molest my sister and me, and so I began to resent his presence and hate him.

He then moved away. I went off to school in Europe, and I didn't see him for another seven years. But I held on to my hatred and it grew inside me. Later I returned to South America, where I became engaged to a childhood friend. At this point, my father asked me to meet with him, but I refused. In no way did I want to meet him. My fiancé insisted. He said that I could not refuse such a meeting, and that I had to respond to his longing for reconciliation. It cost me a real battle, but in the end I agreed, and we knelt down in prayer to ask for God's help. Peace came into my heart.

We met my father in a café, and before I had said anything he turned to me, broken, and asked for my forgiveness. I was deeply moved, and I realized that to hold on to my hatred any longer would be a sin. I also saw that my anger had closed the door to God and his forgiveness and love in my own life.

Child abuse is perhaps the most difficult thing in the world to forgive. The victim – the child – is always completely innocent, whereas the perpetrator – the adult – is always completely guilty. And why should the innocent forgive the guilty? Sadly, many victims of child abuse mistakenly believe that they are in some way at fault, that they brought on or even deserved the abuse. For them, forgiving seems to imply that this is indeed the case.

Nothing, of course, could be further from the truth. Forgiveness is necessary simply because both victim and victimizer are prisoners to a shared darkness, and both will remain bound in this darkness until someone opens the door. Forgiveness is the only way out, and even if our adversary chooses to remain in the darkness, that should not hold us back. If we leave the door open for him, he may even follow us into the light.

KATE, A BRUDERHOF GRANDMOTHER, was also abused as a child. But once she was able to face her own feelings, she found she could reconcile with her mother, who then had a change of heart:

> I was born in a small Canadian town shortly after World War II, the oldest child of a family of Russian Mennonite background. We were small farmers in a homesteading village, and conditions were extremely primitive.
> In my very early years I remember going to church, but by the time I started school this had already stopped. After my father sold our farm, he had to go into the city every day to work. Father's construction job was twenty-five miles away, and after his twelve-hour workday he still had to work the small piece of land that was left to us.
> We were four children, all girls. There were underlying tensions in our family, but we couldn't explain them. When my brother was born, nine years after me, things became worse. Mother stayed home less and less. We didn't realize it then, but she had started drinking.

Soon Kate's mother began to come home drunk, and after that her parents separated. There was no family life to speak of; the house was neglected, and the laundry was never washed. Everything depended on thirteen-year-old Kate.

When Jamie, the youngest, started school, Mother was almost never at home. I never managed to do any homework and was not learning very much. I completely failed ninth grade and had to repeat it the following year.

My two younger sisters left home, found jobs, and shared an apartment in town. But I stayed at home. Somebody had to look after the little ones. And as poorly as I did it, at least they were given something to eat.

In our town, hospitals for mentally and physically handicapped adults were crowded, and the government began to farm out people who didn't need full-time care to local families. This seemed a good source of income for our family, and Mother took in two older men and a woman.

I had to give up my bed to one of the men and share a double bed with the woman, who very often didn't sleep, but when I told Mother that I couldn't cope with this and wanted the hospital to take her back, she was not in agreement. After all, there was a check coming in every month. She said she would come home in the evenings to help me. But the state she came home in! Then she'd say that if it wasn't for me, she wouldn't be in such a mess.

At first I couldn't understand what she meant, but

later I learned that my parents had been forced to marry because mother was already carrying me. At times she became physically abusive. In the morning, if she asked me about the bruises on my face and I told her she had done it, she claimed I was lying.

At sixteen, Kate quit school in order to devote herself totally to the care of her siblings. Around that time, she met Tom, her future husband; they married two years later. She still remembers the guilt she felt when her mother asked accusingly, "Who is going to do the work around here?" Nonetheless, Kate moved out of the house, and soon she and Tom were raising a family of their own.

At this point I just wanted to forget about my mother. I had my own little family, and I had Tom's parents, who loved my children. Suddenly my mother wanted contact, but I found plenty of reasons for not visiting her. I finally had some leverage, and I was going to pay her back.

By this time my parents' divorce was finalized. Mother stopped drinking eventually; she had come to realize that the combination of alcohol and blood-pressure medications would have killed her. All the same, I was reluctant to have contact with her. I simply could not trust her.

A few years later, the couple moved to the Bruderhof. Kate was expecting another child, and Tom invited her mother to share in the baby's arrival.

I was hopping mad and would have nothing to do with it. I told Tom, "You call her right back and tell her not to come; tell her whatever you want to tell her. This is my baby, and I'm not willing to share it with her." I was quite nasty about it. In the end, I went to one of the elders of our community, and we sat down and talked about it.

He listened to me quietly and then said to me, "If you want to call yourself a Christian, you have to come to peace with your mother."

I said, "You don't know my mother."

He replied, "That has nothing to do with it. God commands us to honor father and mother. Nowhere does it say, 'except under such and such circumstances.'"

In the end, my mother did come. She was not well when she arrived and needed a lot of care. I didn't make it easy for her, but finally we were able to talk. Then, during the last few days before she went home, I sensed that there was something she was trying to tell me. More than that, she even seemed willing to listen to what I had to say to her. She wanted a new relationship (by then I desperately wanted it, too), and she was determined to remove whatever was in the way. At that point I realized she was not even aware of what she had done...I was able to forgive her, and healing came to both of us.

In the loving atmosphere of her home, Kate made peace with her mother. She was able to forgive tremendous hurts from the past, but she also made an important recognition: it wasn't only her mother's lack of love, but also her own coldness that had kept them apart for so many years.

Not all cases of parent-child estrangement are black and white. Susan, a woman from California, comes from very different circumstances, and never suffered real abuse at the hands of her parents. Like Kate, however, she was bitter toward her mother for many years and began to find healing in their relationship only when she was able to forgive.

Ever since I can remember, I have had a difficult relationship with my mother. I feared her angry outbursts, her biting, sarcastic tongue, and never felt able to please her. As a consequence I felt angry toward her – a deep, smoldering, hidden anger that made me close myself off to her. I nursed hurts of remembered injustices from early childhood, of sharp words and a few blows (none worth remembering). I became extremely sensitive to her reproof and easily felt rejected. Somehow we just never had an open, sharing relationship. Instead I poured myself into the other adults in my life, most especially my teachers. My mother resented my attachment to my teachers but was never able to express it. I can remember wishing to be taken out of my family to be adopted by one of them. I can also remember a strong physical feeling of not belonging that would come over me in waves.

In my desire to be accepted, I tried to be "good" and hid my true feelings. It probably didn't help that we were never allowed to answer back or say "no" to our parents or any adult. We were children, and we were to be seen and not heard.

It only became worse as I grew into adolescence. I found more and more ways to subtly act out my anger and do what I wanted to do. I also found more ways to sneak around my mother and in a sense "get back." It contributed in a large part to my having a secret, adulterous relationship with our parish minister, who often socialized with my parents.

That relationship eventually ended, and I married another man, but I continued to be at odds with my mother. It was actually a very strange bondage because I still desperately wanted to please her.

Mom went through extended times of physical and emotional crisis over those years, but I found it difficult to sympathize or even show much interest. I finally reached out to her when she was going through a twelve-step program for alcoholism. We had a wonderful week of sharing. I, too, was open to share, having recently gone through a similar time of repentance that led me to Christ. But the doors closed soon thereafter. I blamed it on her, though I cannot now say why.

Finally it became clear to me that her strong, self-confident, in-control exterior was just a shell for a very insecure person who was nursing a lot of hurt from her own childhood. We were both trying to reach out to one another in our own way, but both of us were afraid of rejection and so our efforts were superficial at best. I'm ashamed to say that I just stopped talking after two weeks.

The breakthrough came a few years later when I was hounded by a friend to listen to some tapes by Charles Stanley, a Baptist preacher. I had never heard of him but was seeking for answers, and so I listened guardedly. I can't remember exactly what he said, but it was the right thing for me at the time. I came to see my share of guilt in the relationship and my need to ask for forgiveness and to give it.

Not long after that I visited my parents to tell them about the Bruderhof and of my intention to seek membership. When I was alone with my mother I asked her forgiveness for my actions in the past and I told her I forgave her too. I admitted that I had been angry at her all of my life, even though I wasn't sure why. She didn't understand why I should be angry, but she too apologized for the hurt she had caused. She said, "What has happened has happened, and I can't change that; but we have to move on now." It was a healing for both of us. It allowed me to open up, to be honest, and to express my heart's desire to love and to be loved for who I was, not for what I thought I could give.

The irony of the whole thing was that several months later, at my aunt's house, we were watching TV and Charles Stanley came onto the screen. Like the two proper Episcopalians they are, Mom and my aunt groaned, "Not him!" and leapt to switch the channel. I could feel God smiling with me.

As soon as they faced their anger, Susan and her mother were able to start rebuilding their relationship. Many others with similar stories continue to suffer needlessly, because they cannot forgive. It does not matter who we are or where we are from. What does matter is that we forgive, and that we open ourselves to God's working. Then miracles can happen. Painful memories may still arise on occasion to muddy the water, but we cannot allow them to cloud our vision forever. Even if forgetting is not possible, we must believe that forgiveness is. In forgiving we find true healing.

HISTORY SAYS, *Don't hope*
*On this side of the grave.*
But then, once in a lifetime
The longed-for tidal wave
Of justice can rise up,
And hope and history rhyme.

So hope for a great sea-change
On the far side of revenge.
Believe that a further shore
Is reachable from here.
Believe in miracles
And cures and healing wells.

*Seamus Heaney*

# CHAPTER SEVEN

THE WORD "CLOSURE" has become part of our every-day vocabulary. Frequently used by journalists, lawyers, and crime victims alike, it is often understood to mean the end to a painful, horrible experience. We are led to believe that it can be reached by arresting the criminal, determining his motive, and finally taking vengeance. But can "closure" in this sense really bring peace of heart? What about the role of forgiveness?

Bill Chadwick of Baton Rouge, Louisiana, writes:

My twenty-one-year-old son Michael was killed instantly on October 23, 1993, in a car crash. His best friend, who was in the back seat, was also killed. The driver, who had been drinking heavily and was speeding recklessly, received minor injuries; he was subsequently charged with two counts of vehicular homicide. Michael had only a trace of alcohol in his system, and his best friend had none.

The wheels of justice grind very slowly. The courts took more than a year to find the case against the driver. We attended hearing after hearing, and each time the case was delayed. There was even an

Bill and Michael Chadwick, 1993

attempt by the defense attorney to discredit the findings of the blood-alcohol tests, although this was unsuccessful. Finally, the defendant pleaded guilty and was sentenced to six years per count, to be served concurrently.

We suggested to the probation office that a boot-camp-style program might be of benefit to him – we really weren't out to hurt him, but we believed he needed to pay for what he had done. All the same, we received a pretty ugly letter from his mother suggesting that we had somehow pushed for the maximum sentence...She said that if it had been her son who died, with Michael driving, she would not have held a grudge. I suggested that until her son were actually dead, she should not talk about what she would or wouldn't do...

Her son was finally sentenced to six months in boot-camp, with the rest of his six-year sentence to be served on intensive parole. In six months, her son was coming home. Ours was not.

I guess I had bought into the belief that, somehow, things would be different after the driver had been brought to justice. I think that is what people mean when they talk about "getting closure." We think that if there is someone to blame, then we can put the matter to rest. It's sort of like thinking that if it somehow makes sense, or if the victims get some sort of justice, then the pain will finally go away. In the years since Michael's death, I have read countless accounts of bereaved people who are looking for closure of this sort. I have even seen them on the Oprah Winfrey show, shouting for the death penalty, as if having the perpetrator dead would somehow help...

I was angry at the driver, of course. But I was angry at Michael, too. After all, he had made some really bad decisions that night; he had put his life in jeopardy. I had to go through this anger in order to come to grips with my feelings. However, even after the sentencing, I did not find closure. What I did have was the same big hole in my soul – and nothing to fill it with.

It was some months later that it hit me: until I could forgive the driver, I would not get the closure I was looking for. Forgiving is different from removing responsibility. The driver was still responsible for Michael's death, but I had to forgive him before I could let the incident go. No amount of punishment could ever even the score. I had to be willing to forgive without the score being even. And this process of forgiveness did not really involve the driver – it involved me. It was a process that I had to go through; I had to change, no matter what he did.

The road to forgiveness was long and painful. I had to forgive more than just the driver. I had to forgive Michael, and God (for allowing it to happen), and myself. Ultimately, it was my inability to forgive myself that was the most difficult. There were many times in my own life I had driven Michael places when I myself was under the influence of alcohol. But that was the key to my forgiveness – to forgive myself. My anger at other people was just my own fear turned outward. I had projected my own guilt onto others – the driver, the courts, God, Michael – so that I would not have to look at myself. And it wasn't until I could see my part in this that my outlook could change.

This is what I learned: that the closure we seek comes in forgiving. And this closure is really up to us, because the power to forgive lies not outside us, but within our own souls.

Michael's father learned what may be the most painful lesson for any parent. Yet it is one that each of us needs to learn, whatever our situation in life. Unless we have forgiveness in our hearts toward those who harm us, we will find no peace, however "right" we may be in claiming retribution.

In a society that places a premium on revenge, this is hardly a popular idea. Increasingly, vindication by a court is no longer enough; people want a personal role in the act of retribution. Several states have even introduced legislation that gives murder victims' families the right to be present at executions. Yet these families never seem to find the peace they are looking for. Their desire to see others hurt by the same violence that has hurt them is never satisfied. Instead of healing their wounds, their quest for revenge leaves them disillusioned and angry.

Forgiving is not condoning. In some cases, "forgiving and forgetting" is not only impossible, but immoral. How can anyone forget a child? Pain, indignation, and anger are perfectly understandable and perhaps even necessary, but ultimately these must yield to a longing for reconciliation. Jesus tells us that we will be forgiven only if we forgive others, and we should never forget how he forgave his tormentors while still nailed to the cross. Only when we are willing to do the same can we begin to fathom the mystery of forgiveness.

GORDON WILSON held his daughter's hand as they lay trapped beneath a mountain of rubble. It was 1987, and he and Marie had been attending a peaceful memorial service in Enniskillen, Northern Ireland, when a terrorist bomb went off. By the end of the day, Marie and nine other civilians were dead, and sixty-three had been hospi-

talized for injuries.

Amazingly, Gordon refused to retaliate, saying that angry words could neither restore his daughter nor bring peace to Belfast. Only hours after the bombing, he told BBC reporters:

I have lost my daughter, and we shall miss her. But I bear no ill will. I bear no grudge...That will not bring her back...

**Gordon Wilson, 1994**

Don't ask me, please, for a purpose…I don't have an answer. But I know there has to be a plan. If I didn't think that, I would commit suicide. It's part of a greater plan, and God is good. And we shall meet again.[9]

Later, Gordon said that his words were not intended as a theology of righteousness. He had simply blurted them from the depth of his heart. In the days and months after the bombing, he struggled to live up to his words. It wasn't easy, but they were something to hang on to, something to keep him afloat in dark hours.

He knew that the terrorists who took his daughter's life were anything but remorseful, and he maintained that they should be punished and imprisoned. Even so, he was misunderstood and ridiculed by many because he refused to seek revenge.

Those who have to account for this deed will have to face a judgment of God, which is way beyond [my] forgiveness… It would be wrong for me to give any impression that gunmen and bombers should be allowed to walk the streets freely. But…whether or not they are judged here on earth by a court of law…I do my very best in human terms to show forgiveness…The last word rests with God…and those who seek his forgiveness will need to repent.[10]

Gordon's forgiveness allowed him to come to terms with his daughter's sudden death, and its effect reached far beyond his own person. At least temporarily, his words broke the cycle of killing and revenge: the local Protestant paramilitary leadership felt so convicted by his courage that they did not retaliate.

EVEN IF WE RECOGNIZE the need to forgive, we are sometimes tempted to claim that we cannot. It is simply too hard, too difficult; something for saints, maybe, but not sinners. We argue that we have been hurt one time too many, that our side of the story has been misrepresented, or that we have not been understood.

Once we decide to forgive, however, we must stand back so that God can work. This is easier said than done. How often we acknowledge God's power to redeem any situation, yet refuse to let go! Perhaps this is because we do not fully trust him, and think that we can handle things on our own. But in so doing we shut the door in his face and cut ourselves off from his grace and mercy.

Many Americans have been moved by the story of Steven McDonald, yet few seem able to understand his act of forgiveness as anything other than a feat of supernatural will power. A New York City police officer and detective, Steven was shot and paralyzed from the neck down in 1986 while questioning three youths in Central Park. He had been married less than a year, and his wife was two months pregnant.

Shavod Jones, Steven's assailant, came from a Harlem housing project; Steven lived in white, wealthy Nassau County. Their brief encounter might have ended with jail for one and life-long bitterness for the other. But even before Shavod had been released from jail, Steven started to correspond with him in an attempt to bring "peace and purpose" to the young man's life. He writes:

The author with Steven McDonald, 1997

Why he would shoot me had never been entirely out of my mind as I lay in Six South, looking at the ceiling. I was puzzled, but I found I couldn't hate him, only the circumstances that had brought him to Central Park that afternoon, a handgun tucked into his pants.

I was a badge to that kid, a uniform representing the government. I was the system that let landlords charge rent for squalid apartments in broken-down tenements; I was the city agency that fixed up poor neighborhoods and drove the residents out, through gentrification, regardless of whether they were law-abiding solid citizens, or pushers and criminals; I was the Irish cop who showed up at a domestic dispute and left without doing anything, because no law had been broken.

To Shavod Jones, I was the scapegoat, the enemy. He didn't see me as a person, as a man with loved ones, as a husband and father-to-be. He'd bought into the cop myths of his community: the police are racist, they'll turn violent, so arm yourself against them. No, I couldn't blame Jones. Society – his family, the social agencies responsible for him, the people who'd made it impossible for his parents to be together – had failed way before Shavod Jones met Steven McDonald in Central Park…

On some days when I am not feeling very well, I can get angry. But I have realized that anger is a wasted emotion…I'm sometimes angry at the teenage boy who shot me. But more often I feel sorry for him. I only hope that he can turn his life to helping and not hurting people. I forgive him and hope that he can find peace and purpose in his life. [11]

Shavod didn't answer the letters at first, and when he later did, the exchange fizzled out because Steven declined his request for assistance in seeking parole. Then, in late 1995, only three days after his release from prison, Shavod was killed in a motorcycle accident on Madison Avenue. Steven continues to preach a message of love and forgiveness from his wheelchair.

When I visited Steven in his Long Island home several months ago, I was immediately struck by his gentle demeanor and sparkling eyes – and by the extent of his incapacitation. Life in a wheelchair is hard enough for an elderly person to accept, but to be plucked out of an active life at the age of twenty-nine is devastating. Add to this a tracheostomy to breathe through, and a ten-year-old son you have never been able to hug, and you have Steven McDonald. But I sensed no anger, no bitterness.

Quietly but firmly, he poured out his heart. He called the shooting a "blessing," a severe test of faith, but one that has drawn him undeniably closer to God and forced him to focus on the inner and the eternal:

At first, forgiveness was a way of moving on, a way of putting the terrible accident behind me. But later I realized that I had been leading a sinful and selfish life, and needed forgiveness myself. It was that simple.

Now, Steven has found purpose and meaning in teaching forgiveness. He speaks regularly in elementary schools, in high schools, and at commencements. And he sees his work as a God-given task. By forgiving and sharing his act of forgiveness, he hopes that people will rediscover God.

Eleven years after the shooting, Steven's wife Patti is still faithfully at his side. They struggle daily with the reality of his disability and its effects on their marriage. Steven must often fight back discouragement, and he has even battled thoughts of suicide. But when I asked him if forgiveness itself was a struggle, he said no – it was rather a gift, a grace.

To forgive when one has been so severely injured cannot be easy. Yet even in the deepest agony we are faced with a choice: to love or to hate, to forgive or to condemn, to seek reconciliation or retribution. Steven might have succumbed to bitterness, but because he chose the path of peace and reconciliation, he is changing lives to this day.

One of Steven's heroes is Martin Luther King, Jr., and during our visit he asked his nurse to hold up for him a collection of the civil rights leader's words, from which he read us a favorite passage:

> There is so much frustration in the world because we have relied on gods, and not God…It is faith in him that we must re-discover…Forgiveness is not an occasional act. It is a permanent attitude.[12]

As we prepared to leave, Steven asked me to pray with him. We did, and his face radiated. I have seldom seen a man so contented, so peaceful and assured of his purpose in life.

Chris CARRIER forgave a man most of us would wish dead. As a ten-year-old in Miami, he was abducted and assaulted by a former employee of his father's and left to die in the Florida Everglades. He writes:

> Friday, December 20, 1974, was no ordinary day. It was the last day of school before the Christmas holidays, and we got out early.
>
> I stepped off the bus at 1:15 p.m. and began to walk home. An older-looking man who happened to be walking towards me on the sidewalk appeared to recognize me. Just two houses away from home, he introduced himself as a friend of my father. He told me he was hosting a party for my father and asked if I would help him with some decorations.
>
> I agreed and walked back up the street with him to the local youth center where he had parked his motor home. Once inside the vehicle, I put down my things and made myself comfortable.
>
> The Miami I knew quickly disappeared as he drove north. In an area removed from suburban traffic, he stopped on the side of the road. He claimed that he had missed a turn. He handed me a map, instructing me to look for a certain number, and went into the back of the motor home "to get something."
>
> As I studied the map and waited, I felt a quick sting in the shoulder, and then another. I turned around to

see him standing behind me with an ice pick in his hand. Then he pulled me out of my seat and onto the floor. Kneeling over me, he stabbed me in the chest several times. I pleaded with him to stop and promised him that if he would let me go, I wouldn't say anything.

I was immeasurably relieved when he stood up. He told me that he was going to drop me off somewhere, after which he would call my father and let him know where I was. He allowed me to sit in the back of the motor home as he drove. Yet I was painfully aware that this situation was beyond my control. When I asked him why he was doing this to me, he said that my father had "cost him a great deal of money."

After driving for another hour or so, he turned onto a dusty side road. He told me this was where my father would pick me up. We walked out together into the bushes and I sat down where he told me I should sit. The last thing I remembered was him walking away.

Six days later, the evening of December 26, Chris was found by a local deer hunter. Chris's head was bloody and his eyes black. He had been shot through the head. Miraculously, there was no brain damage, nor did he remember being shot.

In the months that followed, Chris struggled daily with the insecurity of knowing that his abductor was still at large. He also had to come to terms with the physical limitations caused by his wounds: he was now blind in one eye and could not take part in contact sports. And as any teenager would, he worried about his appearance.

Chris resented public mention of his survival, and remembers wondering how this "miracle" could have left him so miserable. Amazingly, at the age of thirteen, he underwent a change. He began to see his nightmare as a blessing rather than a curse. He realized his injuries could have been much worse – in fact, he could have died. He also recognized that he could not stay angry forever, and he decided to turn his back on animosity, revenge, and self-pity forever.

Then, on September 3, 1996, Chris received a phone call that changed his life once again. A chief detective from the Coral Gables police department called Chris at home to notify him that a man named David McAllister had confessed to being his abductor. David had worked as a physical aide for an elderly uncle in Chris's family. He had been fired on account of his drinking problems. Chris visited David the following day.

When I visited him that afternoon, I felt an overwhelming compassion for the man. David McAllister was no longer an intimidating abductor. He was, instead, a frail seventy-seven-year-old who weighed little more than sixty pounds. Glaucoma had left him blind, and his body had been ruined by alcoholism and smoking. He had no family and no friends. He was a man who faced death with only his regrets to keep him company.

When I first spoke to David, he was rather callous. I suppose he thought I was another police officer. A friend who accompanied me wisely asked him several simple questions that led to his admission of abducting me. He then asked, "Did you ever wish you could tell that young boy that you were sorry for what you did?"

David answered emphatically, "I wish I could."

That was when I introduced myself to him. Unable to see, he clasped my hand and told me he was sorry for what he had done to me. In return, I offered him my forgiveness and friendship.

Chris says it wasn't hard for him to forgive. But he says the media still doesn't understand why or how Chris did it. They admired his ability to forgive, but they could not understand what compelled him. They always went blank when the subject of forgiveness came up; it seemed they would rather focus on the drama of his abduction and the details of his torture. In a sense, this is hardly surprising. No analysis of human emotion, however clever, can satisfactorily explain the will to forgive. Forgiveness can be grasped only by those who grasp the mercy of God.

Chris writes:

> There is a very pragmatic reason for forgiving. When we are wronged, we can either respond by seeking revenge, or we can forgive. If we choose revenge, our lives will be consumed by anger. When vengeance is served, it leaves one empty. Anger is a hard urge to satisfy and can become habitual. But forgiveness allows us to move on.
>
> There is also a more compelling reason to forgive. Forgiveness is a gift – it is mercy. It is a gift that I have received and also given away. In both cases, it has been completely satisfying.

In the days that followed this dramatic meeting, Chris began to visit David as often as he could, usually with his wife and two daughters. The two men spent hours talking, reading,

**Chris Carrier, 1996**

and praying, and gradually the old man's hardness melted away. Then, one evening three weeks later, just hours after Chris tucked his ailing friend into bed for the night, David died.

Chris and Steven's stories show, perhaps better than any others in this book, the contradictions in the mystery we call "forgiveness." We have seen how difficult it can be to let go of relatively small grudges. Yet here, two men who suffered beyond their worst nightmares were able to forgive with almost unbelievable – heroic – ease. But maybe this has less to do with them than with their faith in a higher power. In the end, all forgiveness comes from God. He overcomes darkness with light and evil with good. He wants to bring the criminal and the victim face to face for the sake of peace and reconciliation.

IF ONLY THERE WERE evil people somewhere insidiously committing evil deeds, and it were necessary only to separate them from the rest of us and destroy them. But the line dividing good and evil cuts through the heart of every human being. And who is willing to destroy a piece of his own heart?

*Aleksandr Solzhenitsyn*

# CHAPTER EIGHT

MILLIONS OF CHRISTIANS recite the Lord's Prayer every day. We ask God to "forgive us as we forgive our debtors," but do we really mean what we say? Too often, we repeat these holy words without a thought to their meaning: that when we recognize our own need for forgiveness, we will be able to forgive. This recognition does not come to us easily. It always seems safer, somehow, to cling valiantly to our self-righteousness. But isn't humility – the willingness to see ourselves as sinners – the essence of forgiveness? In the Beatitudes, Jesus tells us that the meek will be blessed; they will inherit the earth. And in the parable of the unmerciful servant, he warns us not to treat others more harshly than we want to be treated:

> A master wanted to settle accounts with his servants, and one who owed him many thousands was brought in front of him. Since he was unable to pay, the master

ordered that he and his wife and his children be sold into slavery to repay the debt. The servant begged him for patience. So his master took pity on him, canceling the debt and letting him go. But when that man returned home, he went immediately to a fellow servant who still owed him a small amount, and demanded repayment. His friend begged for mercy but he refused; he had him thrown into prison.

When the other servants saw what had happened, they were greatly distressed and told their master everything. Then the master called the wicked servant in and upbraided him: "I canceled that debt of yours because you begged me to. Shouldn't you have shown mercy on your fellow servant, as I showed you?" And in anger he turned him over to the jailers to be tortured, until he could pay back all he owed. This is how my heavenly Father will treat each of you, unless you forgive your debtor from your heart (Mt. 18:23–35).

When we see how badly we need forgiveness ourselves, we will be filled with love and compassion for others. And when we realize how deeply we have hurt others, our own deep hurts will fade away.

HELA EHRLICH, a Bruderhof member of Jewish descent, grew up in Nazi Germany. Her family managed to emigrate just before the outbreak of World War II and thus escaped the death camps, but they suffered greatly. Her father died at the untimely age of forty-two, and she lost grandparents on both sides as well as all her childhood

**Hela Ehrlich, 1964**

friends in the Holocaust.

At a members' meeting during which a discussion about forgiveness came up, she spoke of her long struggle with bitterness and her continued unwillingness to forgive:

> I sat down trembling, and as I did it dawned on me that if I looked into my own heart I could find seeds of hatred there, too. I realized that they are there in every human being. Arrogant thoughts, feelings of irritation toward others, coldness, anger, envy, even indifference – these are the roots of what happened in Nazi Germany. I recognized more clearly than ever before that I myself stood in desperate need of God's forgiveness, and finally I felt completely free.

Jared, an African-American college student from Boston who recently visited our community, tells a similar story:

> I was six years old when I awoke to the reality of racism: from the sheltered environment of my home, I was pushed out into the world – a local elementary school just down the road from our house. I went there for only a month before city law mandated that I be bussed across town to another school. My parents were not happy with this; they wanted me to go to a school

where I was known and loved. They owned a farm out in the country, and so we moved there...

My father, a veteran of the civil rights movement, taught us love and respect for all men – white or black. I did not see along racial lines. All the same, I was the only black child in the school, and many of the other children had obviously been taught to hate. Children can be brutal about each other's differences. They may begin with an innocent question: why is your skin brown? But then they start to laugh and mock, because they know that brown skin is somehow different; somewhere along the way they have been taught that it is not "normal."

I felt out of place. I was a fish out of water, and these kids didn't make it easy for me. I especially remember one incident. I introduced one of my white friends to another white kid on the bus one day, and from then on they always sat together but left me out.

Then, when I was in the seventh grade in the city, there was a white guy in my class, Shawn, the only white in the whole school. We treated him as an outcast and taunted him with racial epithets and physically abused him. We took out our hatred of white people on him even though he hadn't done anything to harm any of us. We were angry. He symbolized everything that we knew about white people and their history: the humiliation of our people, the lynchings, the mobs, and the slave trade. We took out all our bitterness and anger on this guy.

I can see now that what we did to Shawn was wrong. We were racist, the very thing we despised whites for.

Still today I pray for forgiveness for the harm I caused him. I ask God for forgiveness, since I can't ask Shawn. And I resolve to forgive the guys who didn't have the heart to love me when I was the only black kid in their midst.

JOSEF BEN-ELIEZER, a fellow member of the Bruderhof, was born in 1929 in Frankfurt, Germany, to Jewish parents of East European descent. Like thousands of others, his parents had emigrated from Poland to escape persecution and poverty. There was little respite from either.

My first encounter with anti-Semitism came when I was only three years old. We were watching from our window at the Ostendstrasse when a formation of the Hitler Youth marched past, singing a song that even I understood: *Wenn Judenblut vom Messer spritzt* ("When Jewish blood runs from our knives"). I still remember the horror on my parents' faces.

Very soon, our family decided to leave the country, and at the end of 1933 we had moved back to Rozwadow, Poland, on the River San. Most of its inhabitants were Jews: artisans, tailors, carpenters, and merchants. There was a great deal of poverty, but under the circumstances we were considered middle-class. We lived in Rozwadow for the next six years.

In 1939 the war started, and within weeks the Germans entered our town. My father and older brother hid in the attic, and whenever someone knocked at our

door and asked for them, we
said they were not at home.

Then came the dreaded public announcement: all Jews had
to gather in the town square.
We were given only a few
hours. We took whatever we
could carry – just tied things in
bundles to carry on our backs.
From the square, the SS forced
us to march toward the San,
several miles from the village.
Uniformed men rode alongside
us on motorcycles. I will never
forget how one of them stopped
and shouted at us to hurry up;

Josef Ben-Eliezer, 1946

then he came up to my father and struck him.

At the riverbank other uniformed men were waiting
for us. They searched us for valuables – money, jewelry,
and watches. (They did not find the sum of money my
parents had hidden in my little sister's clothing.) Then
they ordered us to cross the river, into a no-man's-land.
We were not instructed what to do, so we found lodg-
ing in a village across the river.

A few days later we suddenly heard that this area
was also going to be occupied by the Germans. We pan-
icked, and with the little money we had hidden, my
parents, together with two or three other families,
bought a horse and wagon to carry the younger children
and what little we had managed to bring along on our
backs.

We traveled east toward Russia, hoping to reach the border before dark, but found ourselves in a large forest when night fell. There we were attacked by armed men who demanded we hand over everything we had. It was a frightening moment, but there were a few men in our group who had the courage to resist them. In the end they left with a bicycle and a few other small items.

Josef's family spent the war years in Siberia. Miraculously, he managed to escape to Palestine in 1943. After the war he met Jews who had survived the concentration camps:

The first children freed from Bergen-Belsen and Buchenwald began to arrive in Palestine in 1945. I was horrified to hear what those young boys, some of them only twelve, thirteen, or fourteen, had gone through. They looked like old men. I was devastated...

I struggled with the British colonial occupation over the next three years. I was filled with hatred for the British, especially after they began to restrict the immigration of Holocaust survivors to Palestine. We Jews said that we would never again go like sheep to slaughter, at least not without putting up a good fight. We felt we lived in a world of wild beasts, and to survive, we would become like them.

When the British mandate in Palestine came to an end, there was more fighting for land between the Jews and the Arabs. I joined the army because I was convinced that I could no longer allow myself to be trampled on...

During a campaign in Ramla and Lod, my unit ordered the Palestinians to leave within hours. We didn't allow them to leave in peace but turned on them out of

sheer hatred. We beat them and interrogated them brutally. Some were even murdered. We had not been ordered to do this but acted on our own initiative. Our
lowest instincts had been released.

Suddenly, my childhood in wartime Poland flashed
before my eyes. In my mind I relived my own experience
as a ten-year-old, driven from my hometown. Here, too,
were people – men, women, and children – fleeing with
whatever they could carry. And there was fear in their
eyes, a fear that I myself knew all too well. I was terribly
distressed, but I was under orders, and I continued to
search them for valuables. I knew that I was no longer a
victim. I was now in power.

Josef soon left the army, but he still wasn't happy. He abandoned Judaism, and then religion as a whole, and tried to
make sense of the world by rationalizing its evils. But that
didn't seem to work. Eventually he landed at the Bruderhof.

Here I experienced Jesus Christ for the first time, someone who has very little to do with what is done in his
name. In my heart I heard his words, "How often did I
want to gather you, and you would not." I felt the power
of these words and knew that this power could unite
people across every barrier – people of all nations, races,
and religions. For me this was an overwhelming experience. It turned my life upside down. I found that Jesus
came to bring people together, and that he can heal hatred and forgive sins.

In my new faith, I have experienced the reality of
forgiveness. And I ask myself, how can I not forgive
others when I myself need so much forgiveness again
and again? Most of all, I am filled with the hope that

one day people all over the world might be gripped by the same spirit that has saved me.

Hela, Jared, and Josef all had good reasons for not forgiving their enemies. Humanly speaking they were innocent. The burdens they carried were the result of other people's prejudices and hatreds, not their own. Yet once they could see themselves as fallible human beings, they were able to lay aside their self-justification. In doing so, they discovered forgiveness – for themselves and for others.

JOEL DORKAM, A GOOD FRIEND of mine from Kibbutz Tsuba in Israel, experienced hardships not unlike others in this book, yet his story offers a somewhat different perspective. He raises an age-old question posed by generations of suffering men and women over the course of human history: Are there *no* limits to forgiveness?

I was born in Kassel, Germany, in 1929, the fateful year of the financial and economic crash that had such a decisive impact on world affairs and was instrumental in bringing the Nazis to power in Germany... My father was a journalist; mother an educator. Our family was well off, and life was happy until the clouds of Fascism began to accumulate.

Like many Jews in the country, father did not take the Nazis too seriously at first. How could the solid, cultured Germans fall for that nonsense? But when Hitler became chancellor, well-wishing friends advised my parents to leave Germany.

So my father took leave of his beloved homeland, where he was born and raised, and for whom he had fought in the First World War. Mother and I followed shortly, and we were reunited at Strasbourg. We took with us only a few of our possessions. It was the end of our normal, accustomed way of life; we had become homeless, wandering Jews, without a nationality and without rights.

For me, a curious three-year-old, it was an exciting time. I quickly learned new customs, a new language, and I made new friends. But a year later we had to move again; as German refugees, we were considered a security risk in border areas. We went to a village in the Vosges – another change. My parents had to learn new trades and a new language, to adapt to a very different culture, to do without most of the comforts of their previous lifestyle – and before that, to make a living under difficult circumstances...

A year later, the factory that employed my mother burned down, which necessitated another move, this time to Marseille. Again my parents tried to eke out a living, and they built up a rather precarious existence. We frequently changed apartments, which meant I had to frequently change schools and friends. I never had the chance to form lasting relationships...

Then the Second World War broke out, and everything went to pieces. I was a stranger again, and an alien one on top of that...France was invaded and then occupied by the German army, and soon the Gestapo were making arrests...Our apartment and my parent's business were confiscated and, with the help of French friends, we went into hiding.

Finally my parents decided that our only hope of survival lay in escaping over the border to Spain. Father was just recovering from an arthritis attack and had to walk across the Pyrenees leaning on two sticks, part of the time carried on the back of our guide...

After walking for three days through snow-covered mountains, with father repeatedly begging to be left behind, the Spanish *Guardia Civil* (border police) caught up with us. Luckily they let us through – as they did most of the nearly 10,000 Jews who illegally crossed into Spain. Had we been shipped back to France, it would have meant sure death...

As it was, we were torn apart at the Gerona police station. Father was sent to a camp in Miranda-del-Ebro, and mother to the local prison, and I was left behind alone. I spent the most miserable night of my life alone in a freezing cell, thinking I had lost my parents forever. The next day I landed in Gerona's orphanage, which did little to improve my spirits. There I turned thirteen (the age young Jewish males are solemnly received into the congregation of the faithful) – and missed my *barmitzvah*.

A warm-hearted priest took me under his patronage and comforted me in my hardest hours. He also smuggled some money I had secretly carried with me from France into mother's cell, where she lay gravely ill with dysentery and was unable to buy adequately nourishing food. That money probably saved her life.

After a few months I was sent to join my mother, and together we were transferred to a women's prison in Madrid. I was probably the only male in that place, and Mother had to keep watch on me. We had a separate cell, while most of the other prisoners were kept in big dormitories with twenty to thirty beds. During the day we joined the women in these larger rooms, and walking back to our private cell in the evenings we passed the death cells, where women awaited execution. At night one could hear the shots.

Joel Dorkam

Some time later the whole family was reunited in Madrid. Our living expenses were covered by the Jewish Joint Welfare Committee, but there came a time when we had to make a choice as to our next place of migration, and we decided in favor of Palestine.

It was 1944, towards the end of the war, and conditions in the new country were hard. We shared a small flat with my aunt's family, and I enrolled in a trade school at Kibbutz Yagur and became an auto mechanic. The school had been built for Jewish-German children rescued from Europe, but by the time I arrived, there were no children left to rescue. So most of the students were *sabras,* local kids, and I – with my own background of an assimilated German-Judaism and only scarce knowledge of Jewish customs and traditions – was once again different, strange…

Later I did began to feel at home in the new country and on the kibbutz. I made friends and took part in various activities, like harvesting grapes and corn during the summer vacations. Yet many of my personal, professional, and social ambitions could no longer be realized; there had been too many gaps in my schooling. And it was the same for my parents. My mother gradually taught herself Hebrew and found work at a nearby agricultural school, but my father never mastered the new language.

Once the war ended, life became more or less normal again. I finished school and became a member of the underground *Haganah,* fought in the War of Liberation, and then joined Tsuba (a kibbutz near Jerusalem) with my red-haired wife-to-be Sarah, an Israeli-born *sabra.* I made a solemn vow not to wander anymore: this would be my home for the rest of my life, and here I would live and work and raise my children as part of the collective, and try to help immigrants who had gone through similar hardships.

Looking back on my childhood, I realize that it afforded me many useful experiences, and perhaps some wisdom. I learned (the hard way) how much people depend on one another, especially in times of hardship. I discovered the importance of a helpful deed and an encouraging word. I also came to realize that there are good and bad people everywhere, and that most of us actually are a combination of both.

The present conflict between Israel and the Palestinians is a case in point. We have a very serious, almost insoluble problem here: we claim the country of Israel by biblical and historical rights; the Palestinians by their *de facto* presence...That is history. But what to do today?

As far as I see it, the solution can consist only in some kind of partition by mutual consent, and for that we need to build mutual trust, which is very badly lacking, and which will take time...

In spite of all the suffering the Germans caused me and my family, I still feel attached to their history and culture, which I absorbed through my parents. I have done my best to recreate links with decent Germans.

In the sixties, contrary to the then-current policy of refusing any kind of contact, I advocated welcoming German youngsters in our neighborhood as volunteers, hosting them in local families, and making them aware of recent history. We established friendships with these volunteers, and now we visit them, and they visit us. We maintain an ongoing dialogue and do what we can to strengthen positive, anti-Fascist elements in Europe who protest and fight the resurgence of reactionary movements there.

Naturally, we can never forget the six million Jews – including 1.5 million innocent children – who were tortured and exterminated by the Nazis and their helpers. We may be able to reconcile ourselves with present-day Germany, but how can we forget that in the darkest hours of history, in our time of deepest despair, we were left alone to suffer and die helplessly, without any help from the so-called world powers? Even if we forgive those who live in Germany today, what about those who actively maimed and killed Jews and other victims of Nazi hatred?

If forgiving means renouncing blind hatred and feelings of revenge – yes, that it is possible. But does that require pardoning the monsters who committed the worst atrocities in human memory?

I may forgive those who stood by helplessly, and those who did not dare to speak up. I know how much courage it takes stand up to authority and to oppose the kind of terror the Nazis imposed. But I also know that thousands of righteous people took the risk of helping and hiding Jews, knowing full well they were endangering themselves and their families.

Is it possible to forgive Hitler and his henchmen, his SS commanders and soldiers, his death-camp guards, his Gestapo officials? Is it possible to forgive torturers and murderers who starved, machine-gunned, and gassed hundreds of thousands of helpless men, women, and children?

I can forgive soldiers who fought against us in wars, even if they were wrongly motivated…I can forgive people who fight to protect themselves or to reclaim their rights, even if they are misled. But are there no limits to forgiveness?

As Christians, we know Jesus' answer when one of his disciples asked him a similar question (Mt. 18:21 – 22). Yet we also know that his words were more than a rhetorical reply. Jesus *lived* a life of boundless, perfect forgiveness and love, and it was because of this that he was able to answer so simply and directly. For us, it is not enough to quote the gospels. As Joel's story shows, the age-old riddle of forgiveness must be pondered by every individual; it can be fully solved only within each heart, and by each life.

AT SOME THOUGHTS one stands perplexed –
especially at the sight of men's sin – and wonders whether
one should use force or humble love. Always decide to
use humble love. If you resolve on that, once and for all,
you may subdue the whole world. Loving humility is
marvelously strong, the strongest of all things, and there
is nothing else like it.

*Fyodor Dostoyevsky*

# CHAPTER NINE

IN THE SERMON ON THE MOUNT, Jesus tells us that we should love our enemies – in fact, he says we should "bless" those who persecute us. He also says that we must turn the other cheek and go the second mile; that we should not resist evil with evil; that we must meet violence with peace, and hatred with love. He shows us this most clearly and unmistakably with his words from the cross, "Father, forgive them, for they know not what they do." Stephen, the first Christian martyr, also prayed for his enemies as he died: "Father, do not hold this sin against them."

Ilse von Koeller, a member of my church who almost lost her life during World War II, was saved by such willingness to forgive. Ilse and Ulrich were married after the war began, and in October 1942 their first child, Martina, was born. Ilse was overjoyed. Ulrich was away on the Russian front, and she knew that she might never see him again. But at least she had a daughter.

By 1944 it was obvious that Germany was losing the war. The bombing of the cities increased, and Russian and American forces slowly forced Germany to its knees with attacks from both east and west. As the fighting came closer to Cracow, where Ilse lived with Martina, she and her friends realized that they might have to flee the city.

We wondered where we would hide when the Russians arrived. We rowed to an island in the lake with some other women. There was a shack without windows or a door, but it had a roof. We lived there for some days, but then we were betrayed. Twenty Russian soldiers raided the island. The leader commanded us to listen to what he had to say, and an interpreter translated: "You hid yourselves here because you didn't want to remain in Cracow. You are partisans in Hitler's party. I am commanded to shoot you."

"You!" the leader pointed to me. "Your name, and where is your husband?"

"Ilse von Koeller, from East Pomerania. My husband is on the Russian front." I winced as I said my name. To be German was bad, but to be a German aristocrat, as the "von" in my name indicated, was much worse. In 1918 the whole aristocracy had been shot in Russia.

We had to stand in line against the shack. Five soldiers stood in front of us with their rifles. The leader counted while the rifles were pointed at us. My only thought was, what will become of my child when I am dead? I took my baby in my arms; she had to be killed with me. She could not be left alone in the hands of these brutal soldiers. I pressed her to my heart. Then I looked calmly at the leader. Without hatred or fear, without asking for pity, I whispered, "I am ready. Do what is your duty."

The leader watched me and Martina. His expression changed. Whereas only seconds earlier he had been rigid and cold, he now looked almost lovingly at my baby. Was this not the same warm, kind look I had seen in my husband's eyes as he had gone off to the war?

The leader spoke to his men and they lowered their rifles and turned aside. The interpreter said, "This child has saved your life." At once, my bottled-up tension burst. I broke down. My knees collapsed; I was trembling from head to foot, my teeth chattering. I couldn't stop. I wasn't able to speak. I felt completely empty. A soldier tried to calm me down and offered me a cigarette, but I wasn't able to take it – my hands were shaking.

Then the leader commanded his men to leave the island, and we watched them as they rowed away, greatly relieved. I could not hate them or curse them. Rather, I felt a strange compassion for these men.

In the following months, Ilse faced many more dangers. But help often came in unexpected and inconceivable ways:

Once, a drunken soldier pulled me down to the ground by force. I shoved him away with all my might. His face – coarse and full of lust, and so near to mine – overwhelmed me with horror and disgust. I wanted so very much to hate him, to curse him, but in his face I suddenly saw the suffering of all mankind. A deep feeling of compassion overpowered me, a feeling I had never

known before. Was he not also a victim of this dreadful,
merciless war?

The soldier noticed my stillness and was amazed. His
arms, which had been holding me as tight as iron, loos-
ened a little – and in that instant I was able to free myself
and dash away. Furiously he shouted after me, *"Frau
komm, Frau komm!"* Every Russian soldier knew these
words. Bullets hissed, but I escaped unharmed.

The von Koellers survived the war, and Ulrich died after a
long illness in the 1970s. But Ilse's trials were not yet over.
In 1984 a tumor was discovered at the base of her brain. It
was benign, but surgery to remove it left one side of her face
paralyzed. Once a striking woman, she now suffered facial
disfigurement, had trouble swallowing, and was unable to
control her tongue while speaking. As always, however,
she staunchly accepted her lot and refused to admit defeat.
When the surgeon apologized for the effects of the opera-

Ulrich and Ilse von Koeller and their daughters, mid 1950s

tion, she answered, "I forgive you." Ilse lived eleven more years, brave and cheerful to the end.

MANY PEOPLE ridicule Jesus's command to forgive our enemies as self-destructive foolishness. How can we embrace those who seek to harm or destroy us? Jesus's love knows no limits. It extends far beyond the boundaries of human justice or fairness. It engulfs everything in its path, both good and evil, and transforms and redeems every otherwise hopeless situation. When we love someone who hates us, we are not speaking of love as a wavering, human emotion but of a divine power that supersedes our human response to fight back – a love that heaps coals of fire, so to speak, on our enemy's head.

In the spring of 1965 I marched in Marion, Alabama, with Martin Luther King Jr. and experienced firsthand his deep love and humility in the face of terrible injustice. I had been visiting old friends at the Tuskegee Institute when we heard of the death of Jimmie Lee Jackson, a young man who had been shot eight days earlier when a rally at a church in Marion was broken up by police. State troopers from all over central Alabama had converged on the town and beaten the protesters with clubs as they poured out onto the streets.

Bystanders later described a scene of utter chaos in which white onlookers smashed cameras and shot out street lights while police officers brutally attacked men and women, some of whom continued to kneel and pray on

the steps of their church. Jimmie's crime was to tackle a
state trooper who was mercilessly beating his mother. His
punishment was to be shot in the stomach and clubbed on
the head until almost dead. Denied admission at the local
hospital, he was taken to Selma, where he was able to tell
his story to reporters. Several days later he died.

At the news of Jimmie's death we drove to Selma immediately. The viewing, at Brown Chapel, was open-casket,
and although the mortician had done his best to cover his
injuries, the wounds on Jimmie's head could not be hidden: three murderous blows, each an inch wide and three
inches long, ran above his ear, at the base of his skull, and
on the top of his head.

Deeply shaken, we attended the memorial service there,
the first of two. The room was packed with about three
thousand people (many more stood outside), and we sat on
a window sill at the back. We never heard one note of anger or revenge in the service. Instead, a spirit of courage
emanated from the congregation, especially as they sang
the old slave song, "Ain't gonna let nobody turn me
'round."

Later, at Zion Methodist Church in Marion, the atmosphere was decidedly more subdued. Lining the verandah
of the County Court House across the street stood a long
row of state troopers, hands on their night sticks, looking
straight at us. These were the same men who had attacked
Marion's blacks only days before. The crowd of whites
gathered at nearby City Hall was no less intimidating.
Armed with binoculars and cameras, they scanned and

photographed us so thoroughly that we felt every one of us had been marked.

At the cemetery, King spoke about forgiveness and love. He pleaded with his people to pray for the police, to forgive the murderer, to forgive those who were persecuting them. Then we held hands and sang, "We shall overcome." It was an unforgettable moment. If there was ever cause for hatred or vengeance, it was here. But none was to be felt, not even from Jimmie's parents.

Going to Selma was not without danger. Only four days after the funeral, marchers en route to Montgomery were met with tear gas and mounted police who rode the marchers down and whipped them mercilessly. Three days after that a Boston clergyman, James Reed, was killed in Selma, and later a white woman from Detroit, Viola Liuzzo, was shot and killed as she drove a black man home from a march. (We had done virtually the same thing only a week earlier, when we gave a lift to three women who needed a ride to Marion.)

Years later I was moved when reading about a remarkable act of forgiveness by the children of Selma in those same days of February 1965. Local students had organized a peaceful after-school march when the town's notorious Sheriff Clark arrived. He and his deputies began to push and prod the children, and soon they were running. Initially the boys and girls thought Clark's men were marching them to the county jail, but it soon became clear that they were headed for a prison camp almost five miles out

of town. The men didn't relent until the children were
retching and vomiting. Later they claimed they only
wanted to wear out Selma's "marching fever" for good.

A few days after this incident, Sheriff Clark was hospitalized with chest pains. Unbelievably, Selma's school
children organized a second march outside the courthouse,
this time chanting prayers and carrying get-well signs. We
can be touched by such an act or else mock it; either way,
it is children like these Jesus spoke of when he said,
"Blessed are the peacemakers."

THROUGH JAMES CHRISTENSEN, an acquaintance
in Rome who is prior of a Trappist monastery there, I recently learned of a similar, perhaps even more incredible
happening. In May 1996, the GIA, a radical Islamic group
in Algeria, kidnapped seven of James's fellow Trappists in
the Atlas Mountains and threatened to hold them hostage
until France released several of their own imprisoned com-
patriots. When the French government refused, the GIA
slit the monks' throats.

All France was horrified, and every Catholic church in
France – 40,000 of them – rang its bells at the same time
in the monks' memory. What struck me most deeply about
the tragedy, however, was something that had quietly fore-
shadowed it two years before: the prior of the monastery,
Christian de Chergé, had had a strange premonition that
he would soon die a violent death, and wrote a letter for-

giving his future assassins. He sealed the letter and left it with his mother in France. Discovered only after his murder, it read in part:

> If it should happen one day – and it could be today – that I become a victim of the terrorism that now seems to encompass all the foreigners living in Algeria, I would like my community, my church, my family, to remember that my life was *given* to God and to Algeria; and that they accept that the sole Master of all life was not a stranger to this brutal departure.
>
> I would like, when the time comes, to have a space of clearness that would allow me to beg forgiveness of God and of my fellow human beings, and at the same time to forgive with all my heart the one who will strike me down.
>
> I could not desire such a death; it seems to me important to state this – How could I rejoice if the Algerian people I love were indiscriminately accused of my murder?
>
> My death, obviously, will appear to confirm those who hastily judged me naïve or idealistic: "Let him tell us now what he thinks of it!" But they should know that my deepest longing will finally be set free. If God wills, I will immerse my gaze in the Father's, to see with him his children of Islam as he sees them, filled with the gift of the Spirit...
>
> For this life lost, totally mine and totally theirs – I give thanks to God. In this "thank you," which is said for everything in my life from now on, I certainly include you, friends of yesterday and today, and you, O

my Moslem friends of this Algeria, a hundredfold as was promised!

And you, also, my last-minute friend who will not have known what you are doing. Yes, for you, too, I say thank you and *Adieu* and commend you to the God in whose face I see yours. And may we find each other, happy "good thieves" in Paradise, if it please God, the Father of us both. Amen. *Insha'Allah!*

Clearly, this prior and his brothers were not only courageous missionaries who went willingly to their death. There have been many of those. These men were filled with a spirit of rare humility and forgiving love that can only be described as Christ-like.

F EW PLACES on this earth need reconciliation as much as Israel. I first traveled to this war-torn land in 1988, where I met Elias Chacour, a Melkite priest and Palestinian activist who for many years has worked tirelessly for peace. Our friendship lasts to this day, and Elias has visited our communities twice.

Elias might justifiably be expected to harbor bitterness. A "man without a country" ever since his home village was destroyed in 1947, he has been

Elias Chacour, 1990

imprisoned more than once and endured years of harassment and abuse at the hands of the Israeli government. Yet Elias is one of the warmest, humblest, and most compassionate people I know. On a visit to our British community, he reminded us:

> If I call myself a child of God, if my heart is full of forgiveness to the Jews, to the Zionists, to the soldiers who broke the bones of my brother and imprisoned my father – then I can go to that Jew and tell him the truth to his face, and he will feel that I love him, even if I dislike his injustice...I would rather call him to conversion than change roles and oppress him – God forbid! Love is the message of the Man from Galilee.

NAIM ATEEK, a well-known Palestinian priest at St. George's Cathedral in Jerusalem, shares a similar outlook. He learned forgiveness from his father, who lost everything to the Israeli army in 1948.

When people hate, its power engulfs them and they are totally consumed by it...Keep struggling against hatred and resentment. At times you will have the upper hand, at times you will feel beaten down. Although it is extremely difficult, never let hatred completely overtake you. By the power of God the struggle will go on until the day comes when you begin to count more victories than defeats.

Never stop trying to live the commandment of love and forgiveness.

Do not dilute the strength of Jesus's message: do not shun it, do not dismiss it as unreal and impractical. Do not cut it to your size, trying to make it more applicable to real life in the world. Do not

The author with Naim Ateek in Jerusalem, 1997

change it so that it will suit you. Keep it as it is, aspire to it, desire it, and work with God for its achievement.[13]

BISHARA AWAD, yet another Palestinian aquaintance of mine, heads a Bible college in Bethlehem. Like so many on both sides of the Israeli and Arab conflict, he has been wounded by his share of injustices. Recently he told me about his life-long struggle to forgive:

In 1948, during the terrible war between the Arabs and the Jewish settlers, thousands of Palestinians died and many more became homeless. Our own family was not spared. My father was shot dead by a stray bullet, and there was no decent burial place. No one could leave the area for fear of getting shot at by either side; there was not a priest nor a minister to say a prayer. So Mother read to us from the Bible, and the men who were present buried my father in the courtyard. There was no way they could have taken him to the regular cemetery in the city.

Mother thus became a widow at the age of twenty-nine, and she was left with seven children. I was only nine years old. For weeks we were caught up in the crossfire and were unable to leave our basement room. Then one night, the Jordanian army forced us to run to the Old City. That was the last time we ever saw our home and our furniture. We ran away with nothing but the clothes on our backs, some of us only in pajamas…

In the Old City we were refugees. We were put in a kerosene storage room that had no furniture. A Moslem family gave us some blankets and some food. Life was very hard; I still remember nights when we went to sleep without any food.

Mother had been trained as a nurse, and she got a job at a hospital for $25 a month. She worked at night and continued her studies during the day, and we children were put in orphanages. My sisters were accepted in a Moslem school, and we boys were placed in a home run by a British lady. To me, this was a real blow. First I had lost my father, and now I was away from my mother and my family. We were allowed to visit home once a month, but otherwise we stayed at the boys' home for the next twelve years. Here, with my two brothers and eighty other boys, my suffering continued. We never had enough to eat. The food was terrible and the treatment harsh.

As an adult Bishara went to school in the United States and became an American citizen. Later he returned to Israel and took a job teaching in a Christian school. Looking back, he says:

That first year I was very frustrated. I did not accomplish much and I felt defeated. Very few of the students turned to God and my efforts to change this were in vain. There was mounting hatred against the Jewish oppressors: all of my students were Palestinians, and all had suffered in the same way I had…and I wasn't able to help my students because this same hatred was in me. I had harbored it since child-

Bishara Awad, 1990

hood without even realizing it. God could not use me, and now I knew why.

That night I prayed to God in tears. I asked forgiveness for hating the Jews and for allowing hatred to control my life. And that same evening I felt God's presence…He took away my frustration, hopelessness, and hatred and replaced it with love.

In a society that emphasizes self-preservation and individualism, the act of forgiveness is avoided, if not despised. It is even seen as a weakness; we are taught to assert our rights and protect them, not yield them. Yet Christ gave himself up "unto death." Should those who call themselves his followers not be ready to do the same?

Far from leaving us weak and vulnerable, forgiving empowers our lives and our work. It brings true closure to the most difficult situations, for it allows us to lay aside the riddles of retribution and human justice and to experience true peace of heart. More than that, it sets into motion a positive chain reaction that brings the fruits of our forgiveness to others. When we see our own need for forgiveness, we realize the breadth of God's love to us and know that we must pass it on to others.

IT IS NOT RIGHT to try to remove all suffering, nor is it right to endure it stoically. Suffering can be used, turned to good account, for the glory of God. What makes a life happy or unhappy is not outward circumstances, but our inner attitude to them.

*Eberhard Arnold*

## CHAPTER TEN

WHEN WE SPEAK OF FORGIVENESS, we usually speak of forgiving the hurts we do to each other, or of God forgiving our sins. But there are times when we accuse God, when we hold him responsible for allowing us to suffer without apparent reason or justification. We rebel and cry out: how can a merciful God permit this? We refuse to accept our lot, and turn away from him in bitterness.

Can we "forgive" God? The answer lies in opening our hearts to accept his will. Even if God allows us to suffer, I don't believe that it is his will to hurt us. Rather, he seems to let us endure trials – at times long and difficult periods of anguish – in order to make us turn to him. When we are able to do this humbly, without anger or bitterness, his purpose for us will often become clear.

In my own life I once had to face a frustrating situation at a time I was least prepared for it. I had been on a fishing trip in upstate New York – unsuccessful as far as the catch was concerned, but a welcome opportunity to escape the pressures of work for a few days.

On the way home I noticed that I was losing my voice. I ignored it at first, expecting it to improve within several days. It did not, and so I was soon referred to a specialist, who diagnosed a paralyzed vocal chord. He reassured me that my voice would eventually recover, but weeks and then months went by, and there was no change. His prescription was complete voice rest – I wasn't even allowed to whisper. Until then, I hadn't really worried about losing my voice permanently, but now I wondered if I would ever speak again.

To make things worse, our church was in desperate need of leadership. We were in the middle of a crisis of sorts – a period of intense soul-searching and spiritual renewal – but throughout the weeks of lively and sometimes contentious discussion, I could only sit by in silence.

I yearned to be able to participate in these meetings, but I could not; for the first time I realized what a gift speech really is. I was frustrated and discouraged. I couldn't even talk to my wife and children but had to write everything down for them. To be very honest, I was angry. My anger humbled me, and I could see that God wanted me to be silent, to hear him speak.

Three months later, my voice began to return; five years later, it is nearly normal. But I haven't forgotten those twelve weeks, and I am reminded again and again of my need to turn to God in moments of crisis or frustration.

Andrea, a woman in our community, struggled to accept quite different circumstances: she suffered through three miscarriages before having a healthy child. At times, she found her burdens were too heavy to bear.

Neil and I were delighted to find that I was pregnant after only six months of marriage. But one night just before Christmas I felt intense pain that grew rapidly worse. Our doctor wanted to send me to the hospital, and our neighbor, a nurse, came to stay with me until we left for town. She confirmed my worst fears – I would probably lose my baby. The emotional pain was at least as severe as the physical. Why, God? Why me? Why do you have to take away this tiny soul so soon? What have I done wrong?

In order to save my life, an operation was necessary. The baby was lost, and I spent weeks recuperating. What a different Christmas this had become!

We agonized over our loss and felt alone in our pain. When one of our relatives said to us, "Cheer up! Maybe you'll have better luck next time," I felt like I had been slapped in the face. Luck? We had just lost a baby, a real person, our child!

Someone sent me a card that said, "The Lord giveth, and the Lord taketh away, blessed be the name of the Lord." That made me really upset. How could I thank God for this horrible, painful experience? I couldn't. And I couldn't stop thinking that somehow God was punishing me, even though I couldn't understand why.

Our pastor consoled me: God is a God of love, not of punishment, and he is there to ease our pain. I grasped onto his words as a drowning person grabs onto a pole held out from the shore. Neil's loving support was also a help, and we discovered that our pain united us in a new way. The words, "Weeping shall endure for the night, but joy cometh in the morning," especially comforted me, even when I couldn't feel that joy coming, when it seemed that dawn would never break.

Slowly, with time and with the loving help of those around me, I was able to feel that this deeply painful experience had given me an inkling of the love of God, who cares about the suffering of people and who was right there beside me in my pain. God became more real to me, and I could trust in his love. I did not have to understand or know why suffering and pain had come to us.

Some months later, I was again expecting a baby and hoped fervently that all would go well. It did not. Again severe pain, an emergency trip to the hospital, and an operation to save my life. Again another precious little one lost just after it had come into being. Deep pain tore my heart. From my diary of those days: "I cannot see why; perhaps I never will. I need the assurance of faith – Help me!"

Neil stood faithfully beside me. He had lost a sister to cancer some years before, and what he wrote at the time was a great source of sustenance: "We are separated only in physical distance from the dominion of God, and that distance is perhaps not great." I hung on to that with all my strength.

Slowly, over weeks and months, the pain of loss lessened, although it has never departed entirely. About a

year later we again lost a little unborn baby. Once more
there was deep pain in my heart, but this time no des-
peration over why.

Today Andrea is the mother of a beautiful six-year-old
daughter. Although the memory of her first three babies
brings back a flood of emotions, she is not bitter. She
counts her suffering as a blessing, and feels that because of
it she treasures her daughter more than she might have
otherwise. Most important, it has taught her to depend on
God.

JONATHAN AND GRETCHEN RHOADS, a young
couple in our church, were married in 1995. Like any new
parents they eagerly awaited the birth of their first child.
Alan was born after a seemingly normal pregnancy, and it
was only after he was discharged from the hospital that his
parents noticed something was wrong. He didn't eat well
and his muscle tone was poor. He lay very still, almost
without moving, and when he breathed, he occasionally
made strange gurgling sounds. He was quickly admitted to
a nearby university hospital, but he was three months old
before his problems became clear: he would probably never
walk or talk; he was blind; and he had significant abnor-
malities of the hips, brain, ears, and stomach as well.

Alan's parents were devastated. They had long suspected
that something was wrong, but they hadn't expected it to
be this bad. Right away they began to accuse themselves,

and it wasn't long before they began to question God: why us?

Jonathan tells me he was angry, but on closer questioning he can't say to whom his anger was directed. At God? He hesitates. At the doctors? Without a doubt. At himself? Yes, perhaps, even though he can't explain why.

One of the things you learn quickly is not to compare your child to others. Our neighbor's baby is as heavy as Alan, yet he is only a third of Alan's age. He has no trouble downing a bottle in fifteen minutes. For us, every half-ounce is a major victory. Why? There is nothing to say. Either God hates us, or this is just how Alan is meant to be. We may never know why, but if we are resentful, we will kill any joys we might have had.

When this couple turned to me in their need, I assured them that they were in no way responsible for their son's suffering. I reminded them that while every child is a gift from God, Alan was a very special one; in fact, it seemed he was sent to reveal mysteries that might otherwise remain hidden. We should feel fortunate to have him among us, for he can teach us valuable lessons about patience and compassion, and through this draw us nearer to God.

Although they embraced my words, Alan's parents still struggle to forgive. There are times when they want to run away, when they simply can't face another visitor offering meaningless words of sympathy.

As Alan approaches his first birthday, they are once again faced with uncertainties. Recent developments have

**Gretchen and Alan Rhoads, 1997**

included a tracheostomy and feeding tubes, and on top of that, an appendectomy. How much more suffering will he have to endure?

In a world that offers "early diagnosis" (and subsequent "termination") as the answer to imperfect babies, Alan's parents are witnesses to the worth of every child. He is not, they point out, a genetic anomaly. He is a person who has a great deal to tell us, and they are not about to let him go. Gretchen writes:

> His small hand reaches up through a tangle of wires to find my cheek. As I stoop to lift him from his bed, his eyelids lift slightly and he gives me a sleepy grin...In the eleven months since his birth, Alan has been hospitalized five times; we have long since stopped counting the outpatient appointments. Each time we come home with more questions and fewer answers. More tears, and less certainty. But as he snuggles against me and looks

around curiously, he grins. His acceptance is balm to my heart.

How much more pain can he bear? What new hurdles await us? His tracheostomy has taken away the few small adventures we had looked forward to: bottles, and the chance to explore solid food. No more gurgles of joy, either, and no more cries of frustration.

If he lives, the doctor tells us, he may outgrow the need for these tubes. *If he lives.* The words cut to our hearts, and yet his smile continues to give us hope. He is teaching us acceptance – and thus forgiveness – every day.

WITHOUT BEING FORGIVEN, released from the consequences of what we have done, our capacity to act would, as it were, be confined to a single deed from which we could never recover; we would remain the victims of its consequences forever, not unlike the sorcerer's apprentice who lacked the magic formula to break the spell.

*Hannah Arendt*

# CHAPTER ELEVEN

VEN IF WE ARE FORGIVEN by others, can we ever forgive ourselves? Many people are so tormented by their own actions that they no longer believe in the possibility of healing, but even these troubled souls can find hope.

Delf Fransham, a Canadian Quaker, found freedom from his past by showing love to others. Like many whose stories are told in this book, he was hit unexpectedly by a tragedy that changed his life. Yet in a way, his story is very different: the person he had to forgive was himself.

When I was thirteen, Delf moved to our South American community and began to teach in our school. There were eleven boys in my class, all of us ruffians, and only days after his arrival we decided to put him to the test.

It was a typical Paraguayan day – humid and around 110 degrees – and we offered to take him on a hike to see what he was made of. After leading him at least ten kilometers through the jungle, prairie, and swampland, we finally turned back. Shortly after we arrived home he collapsed with a heat stroke.

Delf was in bed for days, and we had achieved exactly what we wanted: we had proved him a sissy. But we were in for a surprise. The day he came back to school, he said, "Boys, let's try that hike again." We couldn't believe it! We covered the same route again and, sure enough, this time he did not become sick. Delf won our hearts, and from then on we trusted him and were ready to do anything for him. We soon found out that, far from being a sissy, he was a talented athlete. We loved to play soccer with him.

Decades later, and only by chance, I found out why Delf had poured out so much energy and love on us school boys: he had lost a son of his own. Nicholas was born in April 1951, when the Franshams were living in Georgia. Shortly after Christmas 1952 he was playing outdoors when he ran towards a truck that his father was backing into the driveway. The truck was loaded with firewood, and Delf did not see his son until it was too late.

Katie was talking to a neighbor inside the house when Delf carried their little boy in, limp in his arms. She remembers:

> I was beside myself – absolutely frantic – but Delf steadied me. We took our child to our doctor in Clarkesville, who was also the coroner, and explained what had happened…There was never any question about forgiv-

**Delf and Katie Fransham with Nicholas and Anna, 1952**

ing my husband, as I knew I was just as much to blame. Likewise he did not blame me, but only himself. We stood in this sorrow together.

But Delf couldn't forgive himself, and the accident haunted him for years. From then on, he went out of his way to take time for children – time he could not spend with the son he had killed. Looking back, I remember how his eyes often glistened with tears, and I think now that he must have seen his son in us, or what his son might have been. His determination to pour himself out for others was his way of making up for the tragedy he had unintentionally caused. I am convinced that it saved him from brooding over his feelings of guilt and finally gave him a sense of peace.

JOHN PLUMMER, a Methodist pastor whom I have gotten to know over the last months, lives a quiet life in a small Virginia town today, but things weren't always so. A helicopter pilot during the Vietnam War, it was he who organized a napalm raid on the village of Trang Bang in 1972 – a bombing immortalized by the prize-winning photograph of one of its victims, Phan Thi Kim Phuc.

For the next twenty-four years John was haunted by the picture, an image that for many people captured the essence of the war: a naked nine-year-old girl, burned, crying, arms outstretched, running toward the camera, with plumes of black smoke billowing in the sky behind her.

For twenty-four years his conscience tormented him. He badly wanted to find the girl, to say that he was sorry – but could not. At least as a country, Vietnam was a closed chapter for him; he could never bring himself to go there again. Friends tried to reassure him. Hadn't he done everything within his power to see that the village was cleared of civilians? But still he found no peace. And so he turned in on himself, his marriage failed, and he began to drink.

Then, in an almost unbelievable coincidence, on Veterans Day 1996, John met Kim at the Vietnam Veterans Memorial. Kim had come to Washington, DC to lay a wreath for peace; John had come with a group of former pilots still searching for freedom from the past. In a speech to the crowd, Kim said that she was not bitter. Although she still suffered immensely from her burns, she wanted people to know that others had suffered even more then she: "Behind that picture of me, thousands and thousands of people… died. They lost parts of their bodies. Their whole lives were destroyed, and nobody took their picture."[14]

Kim went on to say that she forgave the men who had

Phan Thi Kim Phuc and John Plummer, 1996

bombed her village, and that although she could not change the past, she now wanted to "promote peace." John, beside himself, pushed through the crowds and managed to catch her attention before she was whisked away by a police escort. He identified himself as the pilot responsible for bombing her village twenty years before, and they were able to talk for two short minutes.

> Kim saw my grief, my pain, my sorrow…She held out her arms to me and embraced me. All I could say was "I'm sorry; I'm sorry" – over and over again. And at the same time she was saying, "It's all right, I forgive you."[15]

Later the same day John met Kim at her hotel; Kim reaffirmed her forgiveness, and she and John prayed together. They have since become good friends, and call each other regularly.

Did John find the peace he was searching for? He says he has. Although his emotions are still easily stirred by memories of the war, he feels that he has now been able to forgive himself and put the event behind him.

John says that it was vital for him to meet face to face

with Kim, to tell her that he had truly agonized over her injuries. All the same, he maintains that the forgiveness he has received is a gift – not something earned or even deserved. Finally, it is a mystery: he still can't quite grasp how a two-minute talk could wipe away a twenty-four-year nightmare.

DIANE CAME TO OUR COMMUNITY many years ago, one of those who longed to find peace and freedom from experiences that haunted her. Her journey has not been without struggle, but she has found fulfillment in living for others – especially the sick, the elderly, and the dying.

> To be twenty-two and pregnant by a good friend wasn't something I was ashamed about. It was "my" life, and my peers didn't judge me. A long-standing friendship had dissolved into lust in the back yard of my parents' suburban home on a starry summer night, after a big party and too much drink.
>
> The father of my child helped me out of my "difficulty" by driving me down to a New York abortion clinic. He paid half of the cost and we never talked about it again; the whole thing was "simply a procedure." But details, like the clear glass vacuum bottle, haunt me today, over a quarter of a century later.
>
> All I had to say to the one and only friend who challenged the morality of what I had done was a cocky, "God wouldn't want me to bring a child into this situa-

tion." I used God to justify my wishes…

My parents were upper-middle-class professionals, "good" Christians, but I didn't exactly share their values. I longed for free and genuine relationships, for peace (Vietnam!), and for honesty in all areas (Watergate!) – and my search drove me to rebel against the Park-Avenue, suburban-Connecticut opulence of my parents.

I was on a quest for the peace and love of hippydom, for drugs and drink and sex. I was looking for a life of equality and sharing, and I was living in a commune in the country, doing yoga and eating brown rice and veggies, when a small voice sought me out.

At a book display I ran into two humble, loving people who radiated a spirit that was totally new to me. They were from the Bruderhof, and after I said flippantly, "I'd buy one of your books, but I only have a dollar," they eagerly took me on. That dollar changed my life. The book not only challenged every aspect of it but also gave me positive answers in my search for freedom, peace, and honesty. Soon I realized that everything I was looking for could be found in that radical revolutionary, Jesus Christ. I wasn't seeking him, but he jumped out from every page of that book and called me.

The people who had sold me the book not only believed this but lived it. They belonged to a group that was trying to put the message of my book into practice. I knew I had to visit their community.

On my very first visit I still secretly smoked my pot and my Marlboros. But I felt unthreatened. I told one brother I thought there were many other ways to find

God, and though he didn't argue, I can still see his face as he witnessed to Jesus as the Way and not only a person.

Later I picked up a Bible and started in on the Gospel of Matthew; I discovered for myself the love of Jesus for the sin-sick soul. I felt like I was being lifted out of a black, stinking pit and being offered a choice: to live in the light, or to jump back in.

I had come face to face with Jesus. I was the woman at the well, and he knew everything I had ever done. I felt horrible guilt – yet I knew Jesus did not condemn me. He loved me, even though he hated my sin. And he would purify me from the guilt and confusion swirling inside me.

My one-dollar book had talked about the community as an embassy where the laws of the kingdom of God apply, a place where sin is driven out and the kingdom reigns. I experienced that as reality. No other place could have fostered the inner change, growth, and healing I so desperately needed. Nowhere else could I have been pointed again and again to the cross, away from myself and my agony. And so I joined the community. I was relieved to find out that it wasn't just a "holiness trip" but a simple, practical life there for all women and men, a life in which sin was confronted but also truly forgiven.

At times a cloud of depression still wants to envelop me, but I have brothers and sisters who pick me up and help me to start over again. And these brothers and sisters are there for everyone – especially for people who need love, forgiveness, and hope.

In the Gospel of Luke we read that someone who has been forgiven much loves much. Too often we forget the hurt and the healing that we have gone through and fail to notice the needs of those around us. As the stories of Delf and Diane (in fact, of all the people in this book) show, forgiveness can be more than an attitude. Once it is truly accepted, it becomes a way of life.

DAVID, A VIETNAM VETERAN like John Plummer, is a gentle, quiet man who loves children and horses. In the five years that I have known him, however, I have learned that he is tormented by events that happened more than two decades ago:

> Death is on my mind a lot. The deaths I have caused – and wanting my own death – are with me every day. I joke around a lot with the people I work with. I have to, to hide the pain, and to keep my mind from thinking… I need to laugh. Laughing keeps the blues away.
>
> But I cannot love. Part of my soul is missing, and it seems I won't ever get it back. I don't know if I can ever forgive myself for all of my wrongs. I live day to day, but I am tired all the time – tired. Will it ever end? I don't see how. It's been with me over twenty-five years now.

People like David are often urged to receive formal counseling. They are advised to find others who have had similar experiences, to join support groups, or to attend group therapy. David has done all of this; he has seen more than his share of counselors and gone to group meetings with other Vietnam veterans for over a year. But still he has not found peace.

Therapy is doubtless important, and it is often helpful. Sometimes, however, it stops short of offering a lasting solution. A good psychotherapist can certainly encourage a person to reveal the burdens of his past. But confession is useless unless it is followed by remorse and the recognition of a personal need for forgiveness.

Harvard psychiatrist Robert Coles recounts a conversation with Anna Freud that is important in this regard. Although overshadowed by her more famous father, she was a renowned psychoanalyst in her own right, and even she acknowledged the need for troubled people to receive God's forgiveness – something the best psychiatrist cannot give. Talking about an elderly woman's long and troubled psychological history, she suddenly concluded:

> You know, before we say good-bye to this lady, we should wonder among ourselves not only what to think – we do that all the time! – but what in the world we would want for her. Oh, I don't mean psychotherapy! She's had lots of that. It would take more years, I suspect, of psychoanalysis than the good Lord has given her...I will confess to you: when I was listening to all of this, I thought to myself that this poor old lady doesn't need us at all. No, she's had her fill of "us," even if she doesn't know it...What she needs...is forgiveness. She needs to make peace with her soul, not talk about her mind. There must be a God,

somewhere, to help her, to hear her, to heal her...but I fear she'll not find him! And we certainly aren't the ones who will be of assistance to her in that regard![16]

This point is a vital one: we cannot find forgiveness unless we find God. In the end, his forgiveness can be found only at the cross. This should shake us, but it should also comfort us: Christ died for the very purpose of freeing us from our sins. He alone can bring us a new heart and a new life.

The way to the cross is painful. We must first bare ourselves in confession and suffer the agony of repentance before we can rejoice in its freedom. But this freedom is worth everything. It brings the peace that, in the words of Paul, "passes all understanding." And this peace is there for all of us.

IN THE CONFESSION of concrete sins the old man dies a painful, shameful death before the eyes of a brother. Because this humiliation is so hard, we continually scheme to avoid it. Yet in the deep mental and physical pain of humiliation before a brother we experience the Cross of Jesus as our rescue and salvation. The old man dies, but it is God who has conquered him. Now we share in the resurrection of Christ and eternal life.

*Dietrich Bonhoeffer*

# CHAPTER TWELVE

WE HAVE ALREADY SEEN that it is impossible to forgive unless we recognize our own need for forgiveness first. Actually, mere recognition is not enough: we must acknowledge our faults to someone else.

Despite clear advice in the Letter of James – "Confess your sins to one another" – many Christians today question the need for confession. Some dismiss it as "Catholic"; others stress a private relationship with God and claim that it is enough to tell him our sins. But this is a poor argument: God already knows our sins. Others admit that confession can be useful, but that one can find peace of heart just as easily without it. Yet the peace of these people is often, as Tolstoy says, nothing more than "deadness of the soul."

Sin works in secret, and it can lose its power only when it is revealed. Exposing our sins voluntarily is always difficult, but if we are truly repentant we will be glad to

humble ourselves. And when we are truly humble we will
no longer worry about how we appear to others.

Often our desire to come across as a "good Christian" –
as a strong, virtuous, or devout person – keeps us from
confessing our sins. We avoid confession by trying to blot
our sins from memory, and when that doesn't work we
simply hide them from others. Yet by doing this we only
add guilt upon guilt, and sooner or later our sins surface.

This is not to say we should confess out of fear. The
Letter to the Hebrews describes Jesus as a "high priest" who
sympathizes with our weaknesses, someone we can go to
with confidence. He speaks to God for us in our defense,
and if we confess our sins he will forgive us and "cleanse us
from all unrighteousness."

Nevertheless, we must come to God humbly, and our
confessions must be honest and complete. C. S. Lewis says
it is "essential to use the plain, simple, old-fashioned words
that you would use about anyone else…words like theft, or
fornication, or hatred, instead of: I did not mean to be
dishonest, or: I was only a boy then."[17] People who only go
through the motions of confession will not find freedom.

In many churches, a negative understanding of confession leads people to discourage and even silence others who
want to bring their sins to light. Jane, a woman who recently joined our community from Oregon, writes:

> Shortly before I was married, my husband took me to his
> family's church. I experienced a conversion of sorts and
> wanted to be baptized. But I was not expected to confess
> my sins or to change my lifestyle – I was simply "saved."

And so I never felt cleansed from my past, even though
I desperately wanted to be...The willingness to accept
confession and the authority to forgive sin were completely missing in that church.

Bonhoeffer suggests that the problem with such churches is
their tendency to dispense "cheap" grace.

The sacraments, the forgiveness of sin, and the consola-
tions of religion are thrown away...grace is presented
as the church's inexhaustible treasury, from which she
showers blessings...without asking questions or fixing
limits...Cheap grace is the preaching of forgiveness
without requiring repentance, baptism without church
discipline...absolution without confession. Cheap grace
is grace without discipleship, grace without the cross...

Costly grace is the treasure hidden in the field; for
the sake of it a man will gladly go and sell all that he
has. It is the pearl of great price...it is the call of Jesus
Christ at which the disciple leaves his nets and follows
him...Such grace is costly because it calls us to follow,
and it is grace because it calls us to follow Jesus Christ.
It is costly because it costs a man his life, and it is grace
because it gives a man the only true life. It is costly because it condemns sin, and grace because it justifies the
sinner. Above all, it is costly because it cost God the life
of his Son: "ye were bought at a price," and what has
cost God much cannot be cheap for us.[18]

True grace – Bonhoeffer's "costly" grace – is the freedom
we receive through confession and repentance. This need
not be a complicated matter. Peter denied Christ three
times, but once he recognized his sin, he "went outside and

wept bitterly." This is genuine repentance, and we know that Christ accepted it: he entrusted Peter with the leadership of the early church.

Repentance has nothing to do with self-torment. We must be truly sorry for our sins, but we must also turn from them and look to God. If we look only at ourselves we are sure to despair. Once we have cried our tears of remorse, we must stand back and allow the muddy waters of our hearts to clear – otherwise we will never see to the bottom of anything.

The grace that follows repentance is not just a feeling, it is a reality. Sins are forgiven and forgotten, never to be remembered or mentioned again. Suddenly, life is once again worth living.

Steve, an old friend of mine who grew up in suburban Washington, DC in the 1960s, writes:

> In my search for peace and wholeness, I pursued various religions and studied psychology, but I received only partial answers…Not until I finally saw how sinful my life was did I recognize how urgently I needed to change.
>
> The pivotal experience came unexpectedly, one day in 1983, when I first became fully aware of the enormous avalanche of wrongs I had committed. Before that, this reality had been hidden by pride and by wanting to look good in front of others. But now images and memories poured out of me like a river of bile.
>
> All I wanted was to be free, to have nothing dark and ugly hidden in the depths of me; I wanted to make good, wherever I could, the wrongs I had done. I had no

excuses for myself – youth, circumstances, or bad peers. I was responsible for what I had done.

On one page after another I poured it all out in clear detail. I felt as though the angel of repentance was slashing at my heart with his sword, such was the pain. I wrote dozens of letters to people and organizations whom I had cheated, stolen from, and lied to…Finally I felt truly free.

In *The Brothers Karamazov*, Dostoyevsky writes in the same vein about a man who confesses to a murder after hiding his sin for decades: "I feel joy and peace for the first time after so many years. There is heaven in my heart…Now I dare to love my children and to kiss them."[19]

True repentance spreads; it springs from one person to the next, and has the power to sweep through an entire congregation, town, or region.

The people of Möttlingen, a village in Germany's Black Forest, experienced such a movement in 1844, and it turned their lives upside down. Möttlingen is an ordinary place today, and it was no different then. In fact, its now-famous pastor, Johann Christoph Blumhardt, often sighed about the spiritual apathy that had been lying like a blanket of fog over his parish. But a plaque on the half-timbered wall of an old dwelling attests to the remarkable events that once swept the village off its feet: "O man, think on eternity, and mock not the time of grace; for judgment is at hand!"

The "awakening," as it is often referred to today, began on New Year's Eve 1843, when a young man known for his wild carousing and violent temper came to the rectory entrance. After pleading to see the pastor the man was let in. He told Blumhardt that he hadn't slept for a whole week and feared he would die if he couldn't unburden his conscience. Blumhardt writes:

> I had not expected this man to come to me, therefore I remained somewhat reserved and cautious and told him straight out that I did not trust him, nor would I trust him until I had heard him confess at least some of his sins to show his sincerity. But I could not let this strangely distraught man go without praying with him.

Thus began an awakening that surpassed Blumhardt's greatest expectations. By January 27, 1844, sixteen people had come to the rectory to unburden their hearts. Three days later, the confessors numbered thirty-five; ten days later, there were more than one hundred and fifty. Men and women from all the surrounding villages poured into Möttlingen.

There was nothing of the emotionalism of other "revivals," no exaggerated proclamations of past wickedness or public avowals of repentance. The awakening was too sober and earnest for that, too deeply rooted in reality. People felt an inner compulsion to break with sin: their hearts were pierced, and they suddenly saw themselves in all of their blackness. Horrified, they felt they simply had to break with their old ways.

Most significant, this movement of hearts moved beyond words and emotions and bore concrete fruits of repentance. Stolen goods were returned, and enemies reconciled; infidelities and crimes (including a case of infanticide) were confessed, and broken marriages restored. Even the town drunks stayed away from the taverns. And the renewal wasn't limited to adults: rebellious adolescents submitted to their parents, and previously unruly children joined in the singing at school.

Those who question the authenticity of the Möttlingen awakening need only look at its results to see that it was no fabrication. Although ridiculed by people from other towns, almost the whole village was affected. There was no division between the converted and the unconverted; all felt convicted, and all rejoiced in their newfound forgiveness.

That it was genuine can also be seen by its longevity. In 1883, almost forty years later, Blumhardt's biographer Friedrich Zündel wrote that the time of rebirth had not yet been forgotten – even the children of those involved still radiated joy.

Over the last thirty years I have traveled to Möttlingen several times to visit Blumhardt's granddaughters (my parents, both strongly influenced by his writings, named me after him), and I can testify that something of the same spirit that once swept the town off its feet remains even today.

Was the awakening in Möttlingen an isolated event? And can it happen again? Blumhardt had faith that it could: after all, it started with the confession of one repentant man. If it really was a fruit of the same spirit that came down at Pentecost two thousand years ago, we must believe that it can be given to us, too:

A stream of the spirit will come – only let us wait with confidence!…We are a dehydrated people; the thirst is almost killing us, and people are deteriorating both inwardly and outwardly. But now, because we need it, God will also give it again.[20]

TRUTH WITHOUT LOVE KILLS, but love without truth lies.

*Eberhard Arnold*

WE DO NOT REALLY KNOW how to forgive until we know what it is to be forgiven. Therefore we should be glad that we can be forgiven by our brothers. It is our forgiveness of one another that makes the love of Jesus manifest in our lives, for in forgiving we act towards one another as He has acted towards us.

*Thomas Merton*

# CHAPTER THIRTEEN

CONFESSION IS A TREMENDOUS GIFT, but sometimes something more is needed. It is part of the gospel that the body of believers should strive to keep itself pure, holy, and "without blemish." Jesus attached great importance to this. In fact, it was the first thing he talked about with his disciples after his resurrection, when he gave them the authority "to loose and to bind," to exclude and to reaccept, to discipline and then to forgive.

To forgive on a personal basis is one thing; for a church to pronounce forgiveness of sins is quite another. Is the latter even necessary? Many people today question the need for church discipline. Yet if sins can no longer be confronted by a united body of believers – if repentance is seen as a purely personal matter – can they be truly forgiven? And if the church lacks the power to encourage the repentance and, through it, the restoration of fallen members, what real authority does it have left?

In many instances a wrong can be put right by a simple apology – for example, when we have been short with someone or otherwise lacked compassion. At other times we can simply pray for forgiveness. In my experience, however, willful sins such as deceit or theft must be confessed to someone appointed by the church if there is to be full freedom.

Confidentiality is essential; as a pastor, I promise those who confess to me that I will carry their secrets with me to the grave. All the same, there are some instances where more than private confession is necessary. In the case of adultery, for example, the matter must be confronted by the congregation (at least in general terms) if discipline is to be administered and the sinning member restored.

Other grave sins, too, may need to be brought before the church or at least before a small group of trustworthy brothers and sisters. To use the New Testament analogy of the church as a body, it would be unthinkable for an injury to one part to go unnoticed by the whole: the defenses of the entire body are mustered. So too the sin of one person in a united church will affect every member.

As Stanley Hauerwas writes, "A community cannot afford to 'overlook' one another's sins because they have learned that sins are a threat to being a community of peace." Members of a united community will "no longer regard their lives as their own" or harbor their grievances as merely theirs. "When we think our brother or sister has sinned against us, such an affront is not just against us but against the whole community."[21]

Most churches today shy away from practicing discipline. Unfortunately, because of this, members who stumble and fall have little chance for repentance, let alone a new beginning. Mark and Debbie, a couple from the West Coast, experienced this firsthand in the fellowship they belonged to before coming to the Bruderhof:

> Over the years we witnessed the disastrous results of ignoring sin or secretly hiding it. We lived in a small urban community with several people, one of whom was a single man who had fallen in love with a married woman in our group. Some of us tried to tackle their affair by talking with them separately about it. Yet there was no way to really "bring it out in the open" – we had no mutual understanding or covenant to expose and rid ourselves of sin – and so there was no way to experience clarity or victory.
>
> Under the excuse that "church discipline" was too fundamentalistic, too legalistic, and too judgmental, we opted for the lie that his sin wasn't a very serious matter, at least not serious enough to bring it out into the open. Didn't we all sin? Who were we to judge? Anyway, as the modern myth goes, we thought that what people needed most was loving acceptance and space to fail, not confrontation. We were under the illusion that confrontation not only added to the pain of personal shame and self-condemnation but perpetuated the cycle of

failure. So we avoided it like the plague. Now we see that it was our so-called compassion that did the perpetuating.

Tragically, the man eventually left. Two years later the woman also left the community – and divorced her husband.

Mark and Debbie's experience is surely not unique. As Philip Yancey has said, the church is increasingly viewed as an enemy of sinners, and this is because many congregations deal with sin by redefining it, by constantly shifting their stance so as to keep "good" people in and "evil" people out.[22]

Naturally I cannot advise others on how – or even whether – to practice church discipline. While the church referred to in the passage above was ineffectual in dealing with sin in its midst, other churches err on the opposite side. In some denominations, for example, "shunning" is used to separate the "righteous" from the "evildoer," but the emphasis on punishment rather than hope for redemption has devastating consequences. Other churches reject shunning, but throw out the baby with the bath water, so to speak, and end up practicing no form of discipline at all. Indeed, many congregations today seem to care little, if at all, about sin in the lives of their members.

Every church and every congregation varies in its structure, in its level of commitment, and in its understanding of accountability. (In our Bruderhof communities, we do not practice shunning; the most common form of discipline is a temporary vow of silence and withdrawal from common prayer.) Not everyone will be able to find a church that has embraced this aspect of repentance, and others, even if they do, may be justifiably scared or soured by previous experiences. Yet it must be said that in a united church – a church whose members are accountable and committed to each other – discipline is a great gift: in rooting out sin, it can bring clarity to the most clouded situations; and by restoring those who fall, it can cleanse and enliven the body by purifying its members and giving them new faith and joy.

There are, I feel, a few basic aspects of church discipline that must be considered if it is to be practiced effectively. First, it must be voluntary, otherwise it will only harm the person who needs to be helped by it. Second, it must be practiced with love, sensitivity, and respect – not over-zealously, not judgmentally, and certainly never with gossip. Instead of holding ourselves above the disciplined member, we need to repent with him and see where our own sin might have caused him to stumble. Our goal should never be punishment, but restoration.[23]

Finally, discipline must be followed by complete forgiveness. Once the member shows himself to be truly repentant, he should be joyfully reaccepted, and the reason for his discipline should never be mentioned again.

In his novel, *Too Late the Phalarope,* Alan Paton writes of a respected Afrikaner who, at the height of apartheid, commits the unpardonable sin: fornication with a black woman. When his sin is brought to light, his family is devastated. His friends leave him, his relatives spurn him, and his father dies in shame. Yet a neighbor agonizes: "An offender can be punished…But to punish and not to restore, that is the greatest of all offenses…If a man takes unto himself God's right to punish, then he must also take upon himself God's promise to restore."[24]

There are few joys as great as accepting a person who has been disciplined back into the church. In our communities we have experienced this time and again over the decades. The following stories speak for themselves.

When my father-in-law Hans came back to the Bruderhof after eleven years away, he could not simply join us again: he first had to set several things straight. Soon after his reacceptance into the community in 1972 he wrote:

> In the first meeting I was shocked and speechless…I expected that bricks would be thrown, that the whole assembly of members would jump on me; but nothing like that happened. I was given every opportunity to bring up my questions and misgivings openly, and everyone spoke quite openly to me. But what melted my heart was not just the openness; rather, it was a love that shared responsibility – a love that was prepared to forgive because it had itself experienced forgiveness.
>
> It was not a question of a fight between people, but a fight against the evil that separated us. In short, everyone sat on the same bench. Things were not smeared over in a sentimental way, but even the most painful facts were recognized in the light of love.

Humility paves the way for reconciliation. Without it, we remain deadlocked in our pride, and forgiving is simply not possible. Hans's heart was touched by the love of his church, but what finally broke his stubbornness was the brothers' and sisters' humility and their willingness to ask pardon for where they had failed him.

Sarah, another member of our community, writes of the joy and freedom she experienced when she decided to clean her slate and make a fresh start:

> I felt deeply struck in my heart that my entire life needed to be placed under the light of God's judgment. I could hardly sleep at night; something was hammering in my head: I had to repent! I went to the pastor and his wife and told them everything. It helped so much to do that, even though what I had to confess was sickening. And in the days that followed, things kept coming to my mind but I couldn't wait. I remember running to tell them. When you repent, even the smallest thing is no longer insignificant. I had to get rid straight away of every little thing that came to my mind. I could not wait.
>
> I never knew I would find such a joy in confession and repentance. My heart got lighter and lighter. And instead of avoiding me, the brothers and sisters cared for me and loved me more than ever.

There are times like this in every person's life – moments when we feel struck by our sinfulness and are compelled to change. Jesus stands at our door and knocks, and that is an hour of grace: "Behold, I stand at the door and knock; if anyone hears my voice and opens the door, I will come in and eat with him and he with me" (Rev. 3:20). Jesus gives us this chance so we may be reborn and experience the freedom he longs to give us. He may come a second time, and perhaps even a third, but he also may not, and it is up to us whether we let him in. We can either reject the gift of new life offered us, or accept it with thankfulness and joy.

Clare, who joined us a few years ago, writes:

> When I first came, I looked wistfully at the happy faces around me, because I wanted to have what they had. But I was cynical – I was too educated, too sophisticated to be so childlike. And then, within weeks, I rediscovered euphoria, and I regained the spirit I had lost years earlier through my sin.
>
> The importance of confession, the importance of open, honest, direct relationships, and the importance of serving and giving – these are things the world has no time for! But they have given me joy, and if you don't have joy, then you can't sing; life becomes a treadmill and the gears no longer mesh.

A church that practices true discipline is not a sad or oppressive place. Instead of living in fear, its members live in joy and hope.

AND HE WHO SAT upon the throne said, "Behold, I make all things new."

*Revelation 21:5*

A DARKNESS HAS COME over Christianity in regard to this matter of renewal. We are so easily contented, so quickly satisfied with a religiosity that makes us appear a little more decent. Yet this cannot be all there is to our faith: Everything – everything – must become new. Not just a little taste of something new, but *all* things new.

*Christoph Friedrich Blumhardt*

# CHAPTER FOURTEEN

FORGIVENESS IS POWER. It breaks the curse of sin, it frees us from our past, it overcomes every evil. It could change the world, if we would only allow it to flow through us unchecked. But how often we stand in its way, not daring to unleash its force!

We hold the keys to forgiveness in our hands, and we must choose whether or not to use them every day. We can close ourselves to the greatness of God, or we can open ourselves to him and allow him to work in us and through us. Far too often we refuse to believe that he can work in others whom we deem unworthy – in our eyes, at least, they have sinned one time too many. We readily accept God's mercy for ourselves but refuse to extend it to others. We doubt that God can really change them.

In the last year I have met twice with a man on Connecticut's death row. Michael, thirty-seven, is a Cornell graduate. He is also a serial killer and rapist. No one can deny the horror of his crimes, nor can anyone presume to speak for the families of his victims. To do that would be to belittle or gloss over the immense suffering they continue to bear. But neither can we fail to see that Michael, too, longs desperately for forgiveness and healing:

> I feel a profound sense of guilt, an intense, overwhelming, and pervasive guilt that surrounds my soul with dark, tormenting clouds of self-hatred, remorse, and sorrow…Reconciliation is what I yearn for most: reconciliation with the spirit of my victims, with their families and friends, and finally with myself and God.

Jesus died for all, without exception. And he wants us to come to him, not as good people – "I came not for the righteous" – but as sinners.

Can we turn our backs on such a man? Christ did not turn his back on us, and so we cannot deny Michael peace either, or simply leave him to die. Jesus's love is so great that it reaches out to us before we have even come close to him. Like the father in the parable of the prodigal son, he runs to meet us while we are still a long way off; he embraces us before we have confessed our transgressions or even made clear our intention to change. His heart overflows with love and longing for reconciliation.

We see this love again when he comes upon the woman caught in adultery. Before he has even exchanged words with her, he sends her would-be executioners away. He forgives her and believes that she will "sin no more." In much the same way, he forgives the criminal next to him on the cross: "Today you will be with me in Paradise." How few of us dare to love with such faith! But it is just this leap of faith that we must make if we want to experience the power of forgiveness and let God work. In the end, his love is always greater than our love, his judgment purer and more inviolable than ours.

St. Augustine says that we should not see each other as we are now but as we are meant to be – as we will be when God's Spirit fills us completely and makes us useful for his kingdom. This is true faith: to believe that with God all things are possible; to believe that in Jesus we can become a "new creation" (2 Cor. 5:17).

At the beginning of this book, I wrote about a man who had murdered a seven-year-old girl. I asked, can such a man be forgiven? In the months since I first met him, this man has undergone a remarkable change. Whereas at first he was emotionally numb and saw his crime as the inevitable, if awful, result of society's ills, he has now begun to accept full responsibility for his own actions. And he has begun to agonize over his own need for repentance – to weep for others, not for himself.

Can such a man be forgiven? If we truly believe in the power of forgiveness, we will be certain that he can. We will never condone his crime, but we will not deny him God's grace either, and we will not doubt that even he can repent and be changed. Indeed, the whole world would change if we had this faith!

In the first century after Jesus's death, the pagan Porphyry was incredulous that a person covered with guilt and evil could be purified by a single washing; that fornicators, adulterers, drunkards, thieves, and pederasts could simply be baptized, call upon the name of Christ, and cast off their enormous guilt as easily as a snake sheds its skin.[25]

If this could happen two thousand years ago, why can't it happen today? And if the church could experience such miraculous changes then, why can't we experience them now? If we refuse to believe that Jesus can change men completely, then we do not accept the message of the Gospel – we do not believe that the blind were given sight, that the lame walked, and that the dead were raised. Perhaps this is why the churches today are so feeble, so powerless, and so lame: we simply do not trust in the power of God. For if we really believe, Jesus says that our works will be greater than his. He promises us that when we love and forgive each other, demons will be driven out, and the kingdom of God will be among us (Mt. 12:28).

The transformation of character seen by the first Christians was possible only because of a living faith. They were certain that the church could forgive every sin and believed that through the Holy Spirit they were invested with the power to overcome that which was most difficult, impractical, impossible.

Forgiveness was for them much more than just a personal matter or something that took place between individuals: it was a victory for God's kingdom. For us, too, it must have a far-reaching and eternal meaning. We should expect it to redeem all people and all nations, and we must believe that this can happen here and now.

Mumia Abu-Jamal

# A Response to *Seventy Times Seven*

*After finishing the final manuscript for this book, I sent copies
of it to several good friends around the country, including
Mumia Abu-Jamal. I have visited Mumia, a critically ac-
claimed African-American writer on Pennsylvania's death
row, a number of times and asked him to critique my earlier
books. Mumia's response, below, is significant because it comes
from an entirely different context and perspective than that in
which I wrote the book. While to some it may seem overly
harsh, I would remind the reader that Mumia is not a Christian, and that his words are tempered by the great suffering he
has endured. For the last sixteen years he has sat on death row
serving time for a murder that I (and thousands of other sup-
porters both in the U.S. and abroad) believe he did not commit. I include it hoping that the open-hearted reader will be
stirred to deeper reflection – on the implications of my book's
message, and on forgiveness in general.*

Johann Christoph Arnold

I'VE BEEN THINKING about *Seventy Times Seven* ever
since I finished reading the manuscript a week ago – trying
to find the words to match my inner feelings. These are
some of those words.

I must admit that I am disturbed by this book. The
stories seem to shine on the personal level, yet fall flat on
the political level. The book ignores the inherent imbal-

ance between the personal
and the political – and therefore seems to be a spiritual
indulgence for the powerful.
Let me offer an example: the
story of the little Vietnamese
girl, and the U.S. bomber
pilot who napalmed her.
Touching, to say the least.

The author with Mumia Abu-Jamal

But if the pilot who dropped that napalm is guilty, what
of the Defense Secretary who asked for the bomb's appro-
priation, the congressman who okayed it, the machinists
who built the bomb, the chemist who designed it…the
President and Commander in Chief who drafted the poor,
dumb, eighteen-year-old sap, and who declared all-out
war on a nation fighting to be free from foreign (U.S. and
French) domination? They are outside of the conversation, and therefore neither their guilt, nor their forgiveness is at issue.

They are the powers that be. They are part of a State
that sent some 600,000 men and women to a senseless
war in Vietnam, and can do the same thing *tomorrow* if
it so chooses. Because such powers go unaddressed, there
is an implicit forgiveness, for they are never even called
guilty…

In my mind, I cannot imagine myself ever asking the
oppressed – whether Jews, Native Americans, or any
other persecuted peoples throughout history – to forgive
their oppressors. Who can dare?

I hear you answer: "Jesus!" But when I look at the Jews, I see that it was precisely the followers of Jesus – so-called "Christians" – who became their deadliest enemies, who herded them into the ghettoes of Europe, and when the ghettoes filled, into the ovens of Auschwitz…while millions of Christians stood by in silence. As for the Native Americans…this nation pushed them to the edge of extinction, herded them into reservations, onto the worst lands…

It's easy for folks who live in a virtual paradise, who have enough to eat, farms, land, nice homes, businesses, etc., to preach about forgiveness. But, is it really fair to say that to people who live in hellholes – jobless, threatened by imminent death by starvation – people who are, as Frantz Fanon put it, "the wretched of the earth?" Are they to forgive the fat, well-fed millions who voted for their starvation? Who voted for war? Who voted for prisons? Who voted for their perpetual repression? Who wish, in their heart-of-hearts, that they were never born? Should they forgive them for the repression to come? For the genocide that is to come?

"Lord, forgive them for what they do, even though they and their ancestors have been doing it for five hundred years…" Can your heart embrace such a prayer?

It is for this reason that my heart has been called to political action: to change hellish realities, and to try to transform this world from the hell it is for billions of her inhabitants. Change those conditions, and then perhaps forgiveness can be born.

*M.A.J.*

# About the Author

J. Christoph Arnold has served as senior elder of the Bruderhof (approx. 2500 members in eight communities in the U.S. and England) since 1983. Earlier, from 1972 to 1982, he served as a minister and assistant elder of the Bruderhof communities. He has traveled the world extensively on behalf of the movement and met with religious and political leaders, including Pope John Paul II and Fidel Castro, to whom he presented an advance copy of this book.

Christoph and his wife, Verena, are the parents of eight children and have sixteen grandchildren. Over the years they have counseled hundreds of married couples, single people, teenagers, and prison inmates; they have also provided pastoral care for the terminally ill and their families.

Since 1995, Christoph has authored three books: *A Plea for*

**J. Christoph Arnold with Fidel Castro, Havana, May 1997**

*Purity: Sex, Marriage, and God; A Little Child Shall Lead Them: Hopeful Parenting in a Confused World;* and *I Tell You a Mystery: Life, Death, and Eternity. Seventy Times Seven* is his fourth book. Though at first glance his books might seem no different from any others written on such themes from a biblical perspective, they are hardly typical. Perhaps that is because their message is grounded in truths lived out for generations at the Bruderhof, a community movement based on Christ's teachings in the Sermon on the Mount, and on the practices of the early believers in Jerusalem, as described in the Book of Acts. In a sense, they are more than books; they bring to expression the life and faith of a whole church.

Christoph is managing editor of *The Plough,* the Bruderhof's quarterly journal on spiritual and social transformation. An active speaker, he has appeared as a guest on numerous television and radio programs, and on seminary and college campuses.

# About the Bruderhof

**Basis** Despite all that troubles our society, we must witness to the fact that God's spirit is at work in the world today. God still calls men and women away from the systems of injustice to his justice, and away from the old ways of violence, fear, and isolation to a new way of peace, love, and brotherhood. In short, he calls us to community.

The basis of our communal life is Christ's Sermon on the Mount and his other New Testament teachings, in particular those concerning brotherly love and love of enemies, mutual service, nonviolence and the refusal to bear arms, sexual purity, and faithfulness in marriage. Instead of holding assets or property privately, we share everything in common, the way the early Christians did as recorded in the Book of Acts. Each member gives his or her talents, time, and efforts wherever they are needed. Money and possessions are pooled voluntarily, and in turn each member is provided for and cared for. Lunch and dinner are eaten together, and meetings for fellowship, singing, prayer, or decision-making are held several evenings a week.

**Family Life** Although many of our members are single adults, the family is the primary unit of our community. Children are a central part of our life together. Parents are primarily responsible for educating them, but teachers, as all adult members of our communities, support them with encouragement and, where necessary, guidance. In this way, problems can be solved, burdens carried, and joys shared.

During work hours, babies and small children receive daily care in our "Children's House"; elementary and middle school grades (K–8) are educated in our own schools. Teens attend public high school and then move on to university, college, or technical/vocational training. Some young adults find work in mission service projects and return with valuable knowledge and experience.

Our disabled, invalid, and elderly members are a treasured part of the community. Whether participating in the communal work (even if only for a few hours a day) or remaining at home, where they are often visited by children, they enrich our life in a vital way.

**Work**  Our life is a joyful one, as full of the sounds of song and play as of work. We earn our living by manufacturing and selling Community Playthings (a line of play equipment and furniture for children) and Rifton Equipment for People with Disabilities. Our work is far more than a business venture, however. From washing clothes and dishes to assembling products in our workshops or caring for children, it is a practical expression of our love for one another.

**Roots**  The roots of the Bruderhof go back to the time of the Radical Reformation of early 16th-century Europe, when thousands of so-called Anabaptists left the institutional church to seek a life of simplicity, brotherhood, and nonviolence. One branch of this dissident movement, known as Hutterites after their leader Jakob Hutter, settled in communal villages or Bruderhofs ("place of brothers") in Moravia. Here their excellent craftsmanship, their advanced medical skills, their agricultural successes, and their progressive schools brought them widespread renown.

**Recent History**  In 1920, Eberhard Arnold, a well-known lecturer and writer, left the security of his Berlin career and moved with his wife and children to Sannerz, a tiny German village, to found a small community based on the practices of the early church. Though the Arnolds were not directly influenced by the early Hutterites in founding their new settlement, they soon discovered that Hutterian Bruderhofs still existed (now in North America), and they initiated a relationship that lasts to this day.

Despite persecution by the Nazis and the turmoil of World War II, the community survived. Amid increasing difficulties in Germany (and expulsion in 1937), new Bruderhofs were founded in England in the late 1930s. With the outbreak of World War II a second migration was necessary, this time to Paraguay, the only country willing to accept our multinational group. During the 1950s, branch communities were started in the United States and Europe. In 1960–61 the South American communities were closed, and members relocated to Europe and the United States.

**The Present**  Today there are three Bruderhofs in New York, one in Connecticut, two in Pennsylvania, and two in southeastern England. We are insignificant in numbers, yet we believe our task is of utmost importance: to follow Jesus and, in a society that has turned against him, to build up a new life guided by his spirit of love. Our movement struggles forward against the stream of contemporary culture – and against the obstacles our human weaknesses continually place in the way – but God has held us together through times of external persecution, internal struggle, and spiritual decline, and we entrust our future to him.

**Outreach**  At a local level, we are involved in voluntary community service projects and prison ministry. On a broader scale, our contacts with other fellowships and community groups have taken us to many places around the globe, especially in recent years. Mission has always been a vital focus of our activity, though not in the sense of trying to convert people or to recruit new members. The connections we make with others outside our communities – with all men and women who strive for brotherhood, no matter what their creed – are just as important to us. Naturally we welcome every person who is seeking something new in his or her life. Come join us for a weekend.

**Vision** Though we come from many cultures, countries, and walks of life, we are all brothers and sisters. We are conscious of our shortcomings as individuals and as a community, yet we believe that it is possible to live out in deeds Jesus's clear way of love, freedom, and truth – not only on Sundays, but from day to day. With Eberhard Arnold we affirm:

> This planet, the earth, must be conquered for a new kingdom, a new social order, a new unity, a new joy. Joy comes to us from God, who is the God of love, who is the spirit of peace, unity, and community. This is the message Jesus brings. And we must have the faith and the certainty that his message is valid still today.

**The Plough Publishing House** Our publishing house, which is owned and run by Bruderhof members, sells books about radical Christian discipleship, community, marriage, parenting, social justice, and the spiritual life. We also publish a small periodical, *The Plough*, with articles on current issues the mainstream media tends to ignore, and reflective pieces on personal and societal transformation. Sample copies are available free on request.

**Information** For more information, or to arrange a visit, write or call The Plough at either of the following addresses. We can give you the address and telephone number of the Bruderhof nearest you:

**The Plough Publishing House**
Spring Valley Bruderhof
Route 381 North
Farmington PA 15437-9506 USA

Toll free: 800-521-8011
Tel: 412-329-1100

**The Plough Publishing House**
Darvell Bruderhof
Robertsbridge, East Sussex
TN32 5DR United Kingdom

Freephone: 0800 269 048
Tel: +44 (0)1580 88 33 44

**URL: www.bruderhof.org**

# Endnotes

[1] C. S. Lewis, *Readings for Meditation and Reflection,* ed. by Walter Hooper (New York: HarperCollins, 1996), 63.

[2] M. Scott Peck, *The Different Drum: Community Making and Peace* (New York: Simon & Schuster, 1987), 226–227.

[3] C. S. Lewis, *Readings for Meditation and Reflection,* ed. by Walter Hooper (New York: HarperCollins, 1996), 130.

[4] Eberhard Arnold, *God's Revolution: Justice, Community, and the Coming Kingdom* (Farmington, PA: Plough, 1997), 113–114.

[5] *The Imitation of Christ,* II: 3, translated by Leo Sherley Price (London: Penguin Classics, 1988), 71.

[6] Joan Winmill Brown, ed., *The Martyred Christian: 160 Readings from Dietrich Bonhoeffer* (New York: Collier/Macmillan, 1983), 107.

[7] C. S. Lewis, *Readings for Meditation and Reflection,* ed. by Walter Hooper (New York: HarperCollins, 1996), 63–64.

[8] For a more complete account of Bruderhof history, including the crisis of 1961, see Merrill Mow, *Torches Rekindled* (Ulster Park, NY: Plough, 1991).

[9] Gordon Wilson with Alf McCreary, *Marie: A Story from Enniskillen.* (London: Marshall Pickering, 1991), 92–93.

[10] Ibid.

[11] Steven and Patti Ann McDonald with E. J. Kahn, *The Steven McDonald Story* (New York: Donald I Fine, 1989), 133–136.

[12] *The Words of Martin Luther King, Jr.,* Selected and Introduced by Coretta Scott King (New York: Newmarket Press, 1983), 23.

[13] Naim Stifan Ateek, *Justice, and Only Justice: A Palestinian Theology of Liberation* (Maryknoll, NY: Orbis Books, 1989), 68–69.

[14] *Christian Century,* February 19, 1997, 182–184.

[15] Ibid.

[16] Robert Coles, *Harvard Diary: Reflections on the Sacred and the Secular* (New York: Crossroads, 1990), 177–180.

[17] C. S. Lewis, *Readings for Meditation and Reflection,* ed. by Walter Hooper (New York: HarperCollins, 1996), 65.

[18] Joan Winmill Brown, ed., *The Martyred Christian: 160 Readings from Dietrich Bonhoeffer* (New York: Collier/Macmillan, 1983), 64.

[19] Fyodor Dostoyevsky, *The Brothers Karamazov,* translated by Constance Garnett (New York: The Modern Library, n.d.), 373.

[20] Vernard Eller, ed., *Thy Kingdom Come: A Blumhardt Reader* (Grand Rapids, MI: Eerdmans, 1980), 75.

[21] Stanley M. Hauerwas, *Christian Existence Today: Essays on Church, World, and Living in Between* (Durham, NC: Labyrinth Press, 1988), 91.

[22] Philip Yancey, *The Jesus I Never Knew* (Grand Rapids, MI: Zondervan, 1995), 259.

[23] For a similar discussion of church discipline, see the *Catechism of the Catholic Church,* Libreria Editrice Vaticana, 1994, Articles 1440–1448.

[24] Alan Paton, *Too Late the Phalarope* (New York: Charles Scribner's Sons, 1953), 264–265.

[25] Eberhard Arnold, ed., *The Early Christians After the Death of the Apostles* (Rifton, NY: Plough, 1970), 13–14.

# Other Titles from Plough

### A Plea for Purity: Sex, Marriage, and God
Johann Christoph Arnold

Thoughts on relationships, sex, marriage, divorce, abortion, homosexuality, and other related issues from a biblical perspective. **$10.00**

### A Little Child Shall Lead Them
Johann Christoph Arnold

A welcome approach to child rearing based on the biblical idea of "becoming a child" and – building on that – bringing up children with reverence for their childlikeness. **$10.00**

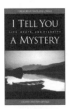

### I Tell You A Mystery: Life, Death, and Eternity
Johann Christoph Arnold

Drawing on stories of real people, Arnold addresses the universal human fear of aging and purposelessness, and shows that even today, in our culture of isolation and death, there is such a thing as hope. **$12.00**

### God's Revolution: Justice, Community and the Coming Kingdom
Eberhard Arnold

Topically arranged excerpts from the author's talks and writings on the church, community, marriage and family issues, government, and world suffering. **$15.00**

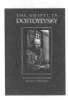

### The Gospel in Dostoyevsky
Edited by the Bruderhof

An introduction to the "great God-haunted Russian" comprised of passages from *The Brothers Karamazov, Crime and Punishment,* and *The Idiot.* **$15.00**

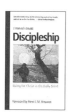

**Discipleship: Living for Christ in the Daily Grind**
J. Heinrich Arnold

Thoughts on following Christ in the daily grind, topically arranged. Includes sections on love, humility, forgiveness, leadership, community, sexuality, parenting, suffering, salvation, and the kingdom of God.　**$16.00**

**Why We Live in Community**
Eberhard Arnold

with two interpretive talks by Thomas Merton. Inspirational thoughts on the basis, meaning, and purpose of community.　**$7.00**

**Freedom from Sinful Thoughts**
J. Heinrich Arnold

Sensitive and encouraging advice for coming through the universal struggle against temptation and unwanted fantasies.　**$8.00**

**The Plough**
**A Publication of the Bruderhof Communities**

A quarterly journal with articles on issues and news items of interest to seekers for whom social justice and the call of the Gospel are one and the same.　**$10/year**

**To order, or to request a complete catalog, call 800-521-8011 or visit our website at www.plough.com. In the UK, call 0800 269 048.**